INTERSECTING COLORS

Josef Albers and His Contemporaries

INTERSECTING COLORS

Josef Albers and His Contemporaries

Edited by Vanja Malloy

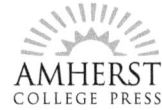

INTERSECTING COLORS

Josef Albers and His Contemporaries

Published by The Amherst College Press
Robert Frost Library • Amherst Massachusetts

This work copyright © 2015 by The Trustees of Amherst College
Except "Josef Albers and the Science of Seeing," copyright © 2015 Susan R. Barry.

All materials herein released on a Creative Commons 4.0 CC-BY-NC-ND License.

You may copy, share, and redistribute this work, under the following conditions:
You must give appropriate credit, provide a link to the license, and indicate if changes were made.
You may do so in any reasonable manner, but not in any way that suggests the licensor endorses you or your use.
You may not use the material for commercial purposes.
If you remix, transform, or build upon the material, you may not distribute the modified material.
You may not apply legal terms or technological measures that legally restrict others from doing anything the license permits.

For more information: http://creativecommons.org/licenses/by-nc-nd/4.0/

Except where otherwise noted, all works by Josef Albers © 2015 the Josef and Anni Albers Foundation / Artists Rights Society, New York. Photography by Tim Nighswander / Imaging4Art. All rights reserved.

Images taken from Josef Albers, *Interaction of Color*, are held in copyright by Yale University Press and made available here by permission. All rights reserved.

ISBN 978-1-943208-00-5 paperback
ISBN 978-1-943208-01-2 electronic book

Library of Congress Control Number: 2015948407

Cover image:
Josef Albers, Color study, n.d.
Oil on blotting paper.
3 1/8 x 11 15/16 in. (7.9 x 30.3 cm)
The Josef and Anni Albers Foundation,
Bethany, Connecticut (1976.2.1374).

Image on page iv:
Josef Albers teaching at Black Mountain College, ca. 1946.
Photograph by Genevieve Taylor; © Peter Reznikoff. Used by permission.

Contents

Foreword
David E. Little — v

Introduction — 1
Vanja Malloy

A Short History of Josef Albers's *Interaction of Color* — 13
Brenda Danilowitz

Explaining Color in Two 1963 Publications — 29
Sarah Lowengard

More Than Parallel Lines: Thoughts on Gestalt, Albers, and the Bauhaus — 45
Karen Koehler

Juxtapositions and Constellations: Albers and Op Art — 65
Jeffrey Saletnik

Josef Albers and the Science of Seeing — 79
Susan R. Barry

Contributors — 93

Exhibition Checklist — 95

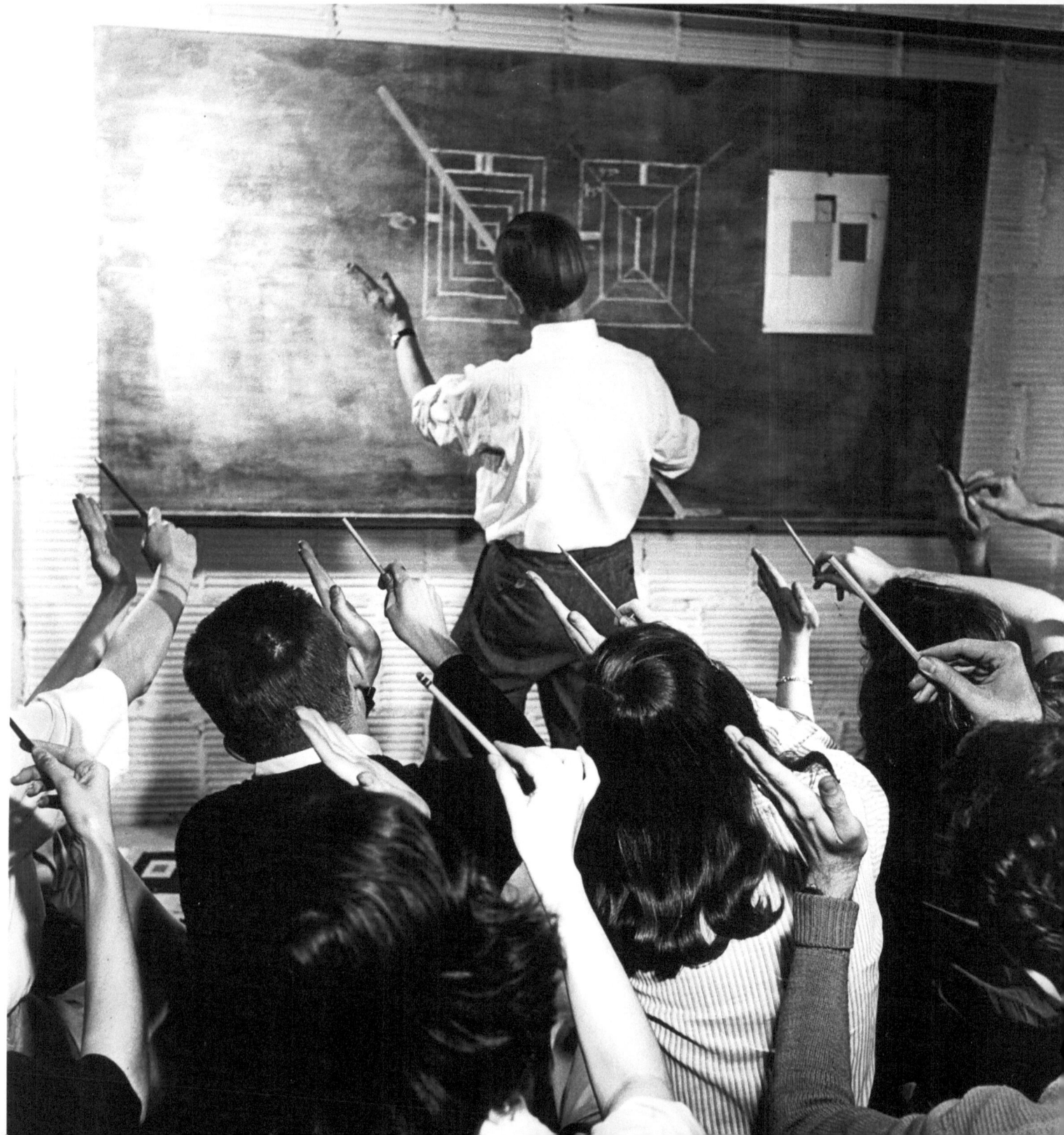

Foreword

Color is perhaps the most subtle and beguiling phenomena interpreted by our senses. Its variations can be profound or invisible—depending on our own biology, or on the culture in which our experience of color has been shaped. We use it both to describe our psychological state and to influence it. We cannot escape it, and yet we often are unaware of how the colors we experience play against, and interact with, one another.

The inspiration for this project, Josef Albers, was an artist of keen perception and a teacher of unique passion. His artistic output inspires a deep contemplation of the significance of color, not just in relation to the experience of art but to human experience itself. The interdisciplinary nature of Albers's concern with visual perception is still surprising us, and a new generation of curators and academics—to which the editor of this volume belongs—is weighing anew his impact in ways that those closer to his own period might not have perceived fully.

It is as a dedicated teacher, however, that Albers has perhaps the closest resonance with such an institution as Amherst College. Surely the transition from the Bauhaus in the urban environs of Dessau, Germany, to Black Mountain College in the rural mountains of Asheville, North Carolina, must have been a bewildering experience for the forty-five-year-old refugee. But Albers soon found himself in a congenial environment at an experimental institution in which the study of the liberal arts was approached with a focus on experience as the guide to education, and on the arts as central, not peripheral, to the liberal ideal.

Black Mountain College did not long survive Albers's departure in 1949, but it seems evident that much of what became Albers's hallmark style as a teacher was honed there. His insistence on students' direct engagement with artistic materials as evidence for contemplating more abstract aesthetic theories, and his guidance of, and participation in, their explorations strike a familiar chord at a college in which student–faculty collaboration is essential to our pedagogy and identity.

Intersecting Colors: Josef Albers and His Contemporaries itself presents a generative intersection of disciplinary perspectives through which a fuller appreciation of this groundbreaking artist and teacher, still capable of surprising us, is offered to the reader and viewer. I am grateful to our catalogue essay authors: Vanja Malloy, the curator of American art at the Mead Art Museum and the organizer of the exhibition; Brenda Danilowitz, the chief curator of the Josef and Anni Albers Foundation; the conservator and science historian Sarah Lowengard; Karen Koehler and Jeffrey Saletnik, professors of art history; and Susan Barry, professor of biological sciences.

◘

As a newcomer to the remarkable Mead Art Museum at Amherst College, I am deeply gratified to be part of an educational institution that is dedicated to bringing together the scholarship of multiple disciplines to bear on the study of the visual arts. Moreover, this exhibition catalogue, as an open-access publication, is available to students, scholars, and readers everywhere. The rigorously researched essays that appear in the publication received the same scrutiny and outside reader vetting of a scholarly print publication. Indeed, this twenty-first-century publication format reflects the spirit of Albers's daring and innovation. By offering such an accessible and affordable publication it is my hope and expectation that new discussions of art, and the ideas and visions of artists, will reach diverse audiences far beyond the walls of the museum.

David E. Little, Ph.D.
Director and Chief Curator
Mead Art Museum

Introduction

Vanja Malloy

> In visual perception a color is almost never seen as it really is—as it physically is. This fact makes color the most relative medium in art.
>
> —*Josef Albers, 1965*

Why is it that the colors of a painting appear to change in different types of light? Or that the same dress can appear black and blue to some and white and gold to others?[1] The immensely influential German-American teacher and artist Josef Albers (1888–1976) was concerned throughout his career with the relative nature of color. His seminal 1963 book on color perception, *Interaction of Color*, does not take the traditional approach of teaching color through theory, but instead provides the reader with visual exercises aimed at training color-sensitive eyes.[2] Albers sought to demonstrate what he termed the "magic of color" through these exercises, which underscore the subjectivity with which our brains process visual stimuli. In an unpublished note found in his papers, Albers explains,

> The physio-psychological phenomenon of the so-called after-image is the reason why we don't see neighboring colors as what they actually are, that is, physically. In our perception, juxtaposed colors change each other in two ways, on the one hand in regard to light, on the other in relation to hue. As there is nothing large or small in itself but only in relationship, so any color appears lighter or darker and brighter or duller in connection with other colors.... This interaction permits the knowing colorist to make opaque color look transparent, heavy ones turn light, colorless neutrals become colorful, warm ones seem cool, and vice versa. It makes [it] possible to make equal colors look different, and different ones look alike, that even defined shapes as well as color areas vanish from our sight.[3]

Among the many color exercises in his book is one named "Intersecting Colors," which inspired the title for this exhibition.[4] In it Albers tells the reader to place a light, medium, and dark shade of red paper next to one another, so that they

Figure 1: "Intersecting Colors" diagram from Josef Albers, *Interaction of Color* (New Haven: Yale University Press, 1963). Image courtesy the Josef and Anni Albers Foundation/Yale University Press.

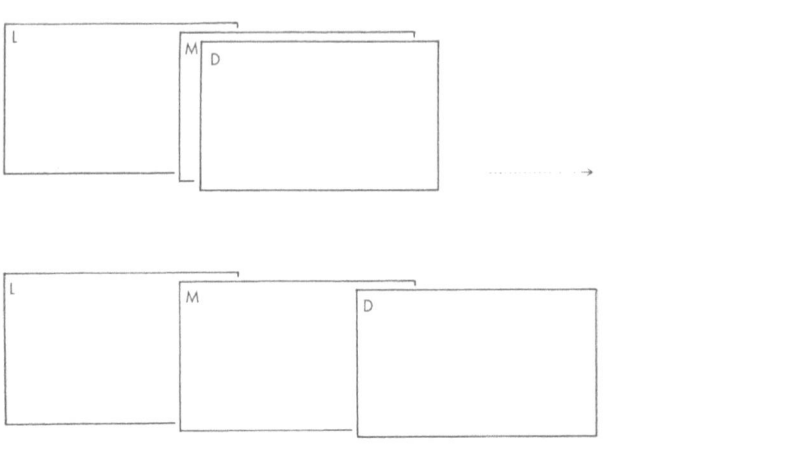

partly overlap (fig. 1). He then instructs the reader to move the darkest sheet of paper toward the right, so that it slowly reveals more of the medium-red paper in the middle. If one looks closely at the middle red during this process, an optical illusion will occur; the medium-red paper will appear to become lighter in hue on one edge and darker on the other, seemingly taking on the properties of its neighboring colors. While common sense tells us that the paper could not have changed color, our brain seems to indicate otherwise.

It is not a coincidence that Albers's concern with the deceptiveness of visual perception developed during a momentous period in vision science. During his lifetime great advances were made in improving our knowledge of how the brain interprets the information it receives from the eye. The American physiologist Ida Henrietta Hyde (1857–1945) invented the microelectrode in the 1930s, enabling scientists to record the activity of single cells in the brain. Advancements in neuroanatomy then made it possible to understand how these cells are interconnected.

Science made equally great strides during these decades in understanding the properties of light. For an object to appear colored it must selectively absorb some part of the visible light spectrum and reflect the rest. Thus our ability to see in color is a result of the way our brains process information about light. In 1905 Albert Einstein published one of his *annus mirablus* papers on photon theory, in which he introduced the concept that light has the qualities of a wave and of particles; that is, light comprises indivisible units (or quanta) of light energy, termed photons, which travel in a wavelike manner. Decades later, in 1938, Selig

Hecht (1892–1947) showed the immense sensitivity of the eye's photosensitive rod cells when he demonstrated that a single photon can trigger a response in the eye. In addition to this improved understanding of the physiology of the brain and the phenomenon of light, advances were made by Gestalt psychologists at the Berlin school in understanding the context of visual perception by studying how the brain and eye create a unified whole from the myriad of visual stimuli in the environment. Thus during the twentieth century vision science had become increasingly interdisciplinary, involving diverse fields such as optics, neuroscience, physics, and psychology.

No doubt Josef Albers was a product of this scientific era. Throughout his long career as a teacher and artist he was concerned with how the appearance of the physical world around us is inherently dependent upon and altered by the mind.[5] Advances in vision science, which were covered extensively in the news and popular media, were certainly of great interest to him as well. In his personal notes, for instance, Albers commented on the twelve-page feature article on color in the July 1944 issue of *Life* magazine and its detailed discussion of light, the additive and subtractive qualities of color, and the science behind visual illusion.[6] Furthermore, while Albers was a professor at the Bauhaus in his native Germany (1925–1933), he developed an interest in Gestalt psychology.[7] After he emigrated to the United States in 1933, Gestalt principles continued to inform his approach to teaching art at Black Mountain College in North Carolina (1933–1949) and the Yale School of Art in Connecticut (1950–1958), where he chaired the Department of Design.[8] According to Alvin Eisenmann (1921–2013), the head of the graduate program in graphic design at Yale, Albers "knew the names of all the Gestaltists. He talked about [Max] Wertheimer's book all the time, and very frequently quoted from it…. He knew that stuff cold."[9] The artist's library, which is now housed in the Josef and Anni Albers Foundation, includes a diverse array of scientific books on color and vision that further demonstrates Albers's wide-ranging interest in visual perception.[10]

The interdisciplinary nature of Albers's concern with vision did not go unnoticed during his lifetime. In November 1965 *Yale Scientific Magazine* featured an "optical art" issue that introduced Albers, along with several of his contemporaries, and proposed a connection between their new type of art and modern scientific thought.[11] In 1970 the journal of art, sciences, and technology *Leonardo* featured an interview with Albers in which the interviewer noted the "considerable application of scientific method" in Albers's art and teaching.[12] But while there was a curiosity by the mid-'60s about the influence of scientific thought on Albers's practices, there was arguably a greater tendency to discount the influence of science on his work.[13] This can be explained in part by the deepening division between the arts and the sciences that arose in academia in the midst of this scientific advancement, and which had its echo in popular sentiments. In a 1959 lecture entitled "The Two Cultures," C. P. Snow famously decried the growing schism endangering communication or even intelligibility between the arts and sciences.[14] Thankfully, a recent and growing movement in art historical scholarship is challenging the extent of that division by revealing the many interconnections and exchanges between the arts and sciences in the twentieth century.[15]

◙

The goal of this volume, and more broadly of the exhibition for which it serves as the catalogue, is to draw attention to the ways in which scientific concerns with visual perception informed Albers's art and teaching, as well as to the work of some of his students and contemporaries. In order to situate Albers within a broader interdisciplinary context, this volume brings together the voices of scholars with diverse areas of expertise, including art history, neuroscience, and the history of science. The first essay, written by Brenda Danilowitz, the chief curator at the Anni and Josef Albers Foundation, provides a detailed introduction to Albers's *Interaction of Color*. Danilowitz compares Albers's experiential teaching methods with those of his predecessors, showing how markedly original he was in both his instructional practices and his understanding of color. The science historian and conservator Sarah Lowengard then offers a new perspective for understanding Albers's *Interaction of Color* by examining its mixed reception by the scientific community, especially in relation to a more rigorously scientific book on color published in the same year. The essay of Karen Koehler, an art historian, examines Albers's concern with context and visual perception in relation to the Berlin school's research on Gestalt psychology. Through this discussion, Koehler provides a fascinating explanation for the visual anomalies found in much of Albers's work and provides new insights into the formative years of Albers's art and teaching. Next, the art historian Jeffrey Saletnik examines Albers's legacy among a younger generation of op art contemporaries, many of whom began their careers as Albers's students. Finally, Susan Barry lends her expertise in neuroscience to reveal yet another side to Albers's work by explaining the science behind the visual effects of his art and teaching exercises.

Inspired by artworks in the Mead's collection, the exhibition incorporates significant loans from the Josef and Anni Albers Foundation, including works that have never been shown in public before. In addition to a representative selection of his abstract artwork (ranging from his early Bauhaus-era glass paintings to his late-career *Homage to the Square*), *Intersecting Colors* includes a selection of screenprints from Albers's 1972 portfolio *Formulation : Articulation*, which refer back to many of his best-known paintings. With explicit reference to his own statements, the exhibition examines the visual questions Albers sought to explore in his art, such as how, for example, the ambiguous form in the painting *Heraldic*, 1935 (fig. 2) can offer the viewer the ability to read the same work in several different ways.

Since the visual effect of his art was based on slight color differences, Albers went to great lengths to ensure that the colors in his prints remained accurate. The exhibition thus includes an example of a painting on paper that Albers cut in half so that he could give one portion to his printer while retaining the other for his records. The corresponding print is also included in the exhibition,

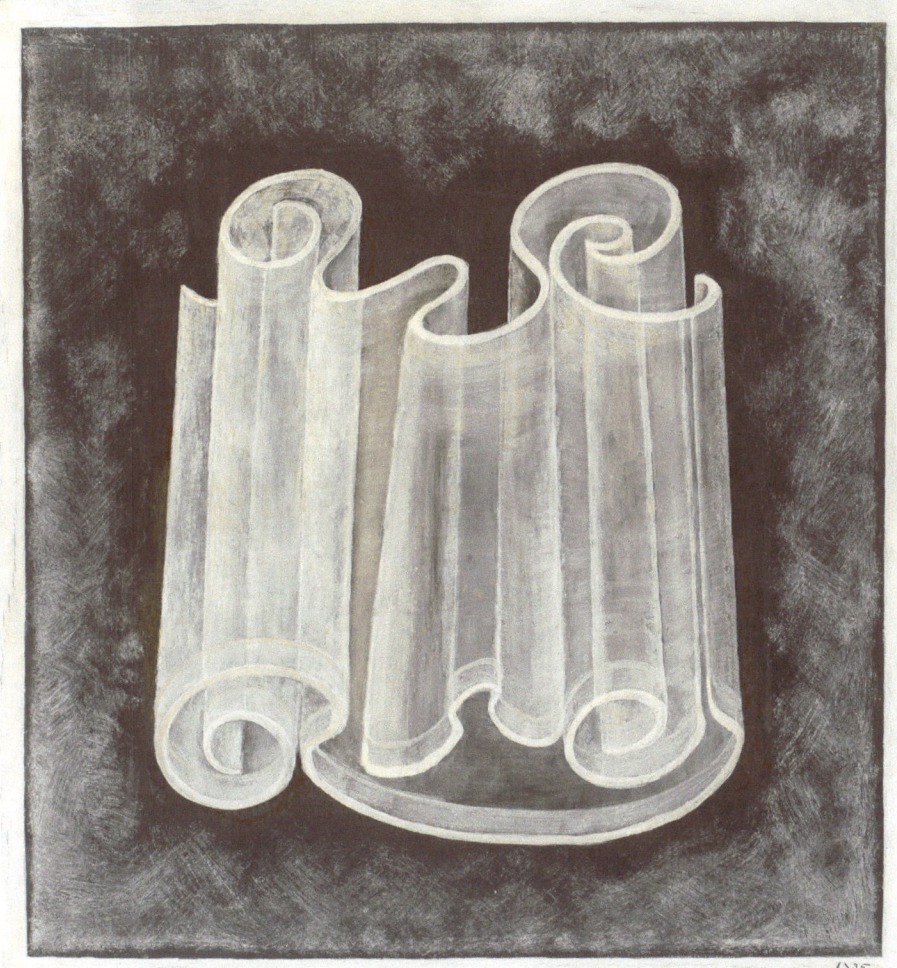

Figure 2: Josef Albers, *Heraldic*, 1935. Oil on stainless steel, 16 3/4 x 16 in. (42.5 x 40.6 cm). The Josef and Anni Albers Foundation (1976.1.1863).

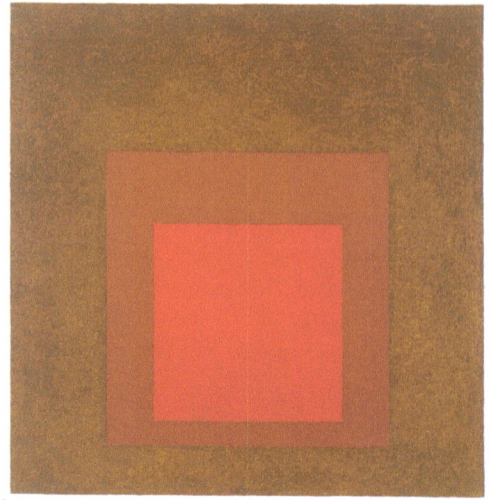

Figure 3a (left): Josef Albers, *Study for Homage to the Square: Rooted*, 1961. Oil on board. 30 x 30 in. (76.2 x 76.2 cm). Mead Art Museum, Amherst College, gift of Richard S. Zeisler (Class of 1937) (1965.93). Cat. 5.

Figure 3b (right): Verso detail of Josef Albers, *Study for Homage to the Square*, 1961. Oil on board, 30 x 30 in. (76.2 x 76.2 cm). Mead Art Museum, Amherst College; gift of Richard S. Zeisler (Class of 1937) (1965.93). Cat. 5.

allowing visitors to judge for themselves how accurately the color of Albers's preparatory study matches that of the final print.

In addition to showing Albers's working process with screenprints, the exhibition provides insight into his use of paint. Albers often painted straight from the tube and took meticulous notes on the paint colors he owned. His written annotations on the backs of paintings, such as the Mead's *Study for Homage to the Square: Rooted* (figs. 3a and 3b), document the paint names and brands in such detail that they often read like recipe cards. His color studies reveal, for instance, how the same color name purchased from different paint brands appeared markedly different. The application of veneers to the paint colors often added an additional dimension, as this clear sheen would change a color's appearance. In the preliminary studies for his paintings Albers produced many compositions exploring different color possibilities and relationships, as seen in two such studies for an *Homage to the Square* painting (fig. 4). Once he had determined the desired color components, Albers would begin painting using a palette knife in place of a brush. This technique gave his paintings a textured quality, a characteristic often lost in reproductions and only fully appreciated in person. Similarly, it is important to note that the colors Albers selected so carefully for his prints and paintings often appear altered when digitally reproduced; this is especially true of reproductions on digital screens, which vary greatly in how accurately they reproduce color. This exhibition therefore offers viewers the unique opportunity to see many of Albers's artworks and color studies in person and to experience the full visual effects he intended.

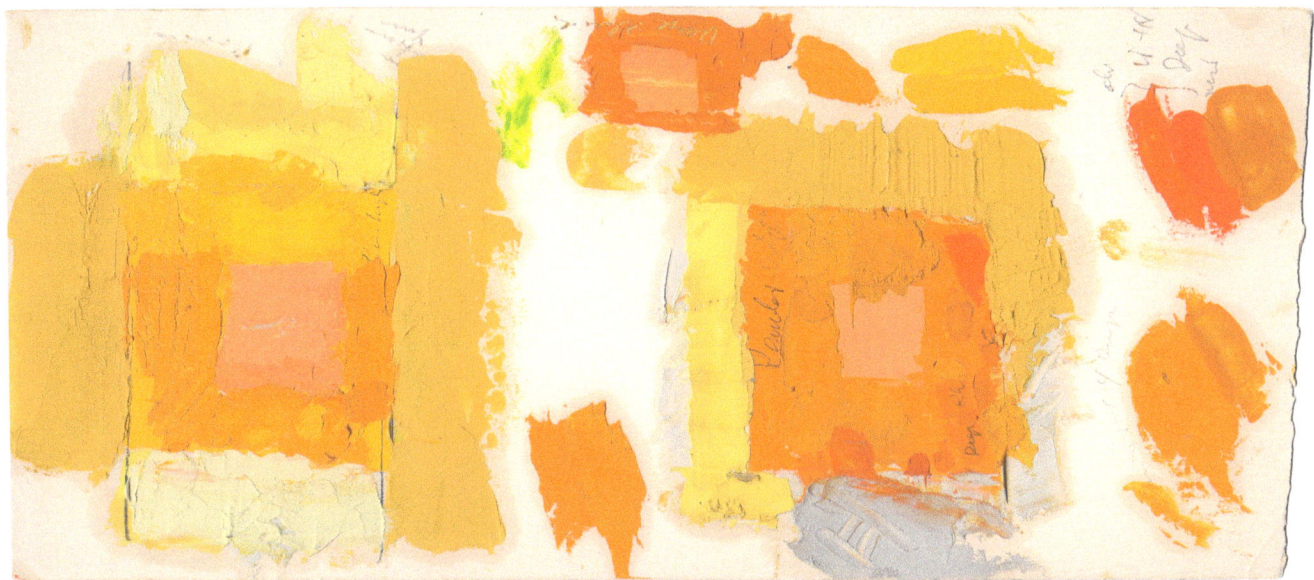

Figure 4: Josef Albers, *Two color studies for Homage to the Square*, n.d. Oil on paper, 4 7/8 x 11 5/8 in. (12.4 x 29.5 cm). The Josef and Anni Albers Foundation (1976.2.1514). Cat. 35.

Intersecting Colors also seeks to examine Albers's lasting legacy as an influential teacher. The exhibition includes a first-edition copy of his internationally influential book *Interaction of Color* along with its recent interactive App, which allows visitors to try their hand at Albers's color exercises. The plates in the book were originally taken from color studies completed by Albers's students at the Yale School of Art and chosen by the artist for the publication. Numerous examples of original student color studies are included in the exhibition to offer viewers a better sense of their original proportions and interactive qualities. The exhibition also contains selected works from Albers's contemporaries, many of whom started out as his students, such as Richard Anuszkiewicz (b. 1930) and Ruth Asawa (1926–2013). Together these works underscore the momentous influence that Albers's interdisciplinary concern with visual perception had on the arts.

I'm delighted that the Amherst College Press is the publisher of this catalogue, and that it is being made available both in print and open-access formats. I am indebted to Mark Edington, director of the Press, for enthusiastically taking on this project and investing much time and energy in seeing it through. I sincerely hope that this is the first of many collaborations between Amherst College Press and the Mead Art Museum.

I am enormously grateful to the authors for their contributions: Brenda Danilowitz, Sarah Lowengard, Karen Koehler, Jeffrey Saletnik, and Susan Barry. I also would like to thank the ten anonymous peer reviewers for their insights and helpful suggestions. Taken as a whole, the essays in this catalogue provide a new, interdisciplinary examination of the work of Josef Albers, placing him within a wider discussion of the connections among art, visual perception, and modern science. I hope that this discussion will highlight the interconnections between the arts and sciences and that it will encourage more explorations of this type.

Such a publication would not be possible without the generous and farsighted support of the Josef and Anni Albers Foundation in giving us permission to include in an open-access publication so many works over which they hold copyright. A critical obstacle to scholarship in art history is the complexity and cost of attaining copyright clearance for publications. While understandable to a degree, this has left a chilling effect on the conduct of scholarly work in the field. By supporting so fully the sharing of these images, the Albers Foundation has taken a position of visionary leadership in both supporting research and, as a happy consequence, significantly expanding the audience of students and readers able to learn about Albers and his influence. I hope their model will be both admired and followed.

The staff of the Josef and Anni Albers Foundation also generously supported each stage of this project. They graciously opened their archives—as well as their kitchen!—to me, and lent the exhibition thirty works by Albers and his students. I would like to thank Nicholas Fox Weber, director of the foundation, for his support. I am especially grateful to Brenda Danilowitz, chief curator, who spent countless hours with me discussing Albers's work and the exhibition, as well as contributing an essay to this catalogue. I am also grateful to Michael Beggs, Fritz Horstman, Samuel McCune, and Karis Medina for assisting me with my research and all aspects of the loan process. Finally, I would like to thank Jeannette Redensek for showing me Josef Albers's library and for sharing her thoughts with me on the subject of Albers and science.

The production of the exhibition catalogue would not have been possible without our exceptionally talented copy editor, Ella Kusnetz. I also would like to thank the catalogue's digital designer, Kris Tobiassen, who did a remarkable job designing the catalogue.

At Amherst College I am grateful to my colleagues at the Mead Art Museum for their support. I would especially like to thank Tim Gilfillan and Stephen Fisher, who managed the logistics of the loans and installation, Sheila Flaherty-Jones, who edited the exhibition's wall labels and press release, and Pam Russell, who organized a wonderful faculty Mellon seminar on art and visual perception to mark the occasion of this exhibition. Jonathan Jackson, Amherst College class of 2018 and American art summer intern at the Mead Art Museum, provided invaluable assistance at nearly every stage of this exhibition. His great work ethic and wonderful talents made him indispensable to this project. I am also extremely grateful to the Mead's recently appointed director, David E. Little, for his unwavering support of the exhibition and catalogue.

I would further like to thank the College's Dean of Faculty, Catherine Epstein, and members of the Mead's Advisory Board for their strong support. My gratitude also goes out to my colleagues in the Department of Art and History of Art for their collaboration and encouragement. I would also like to thank Rachel Rogel in the Office of Communications at Amherst College for her outstanding work on behalf of this project. I am further grateful to Christopher Benfey and Arnold Trehub for their support of this exhibition.

This catalogue was made possible by the funds generously provided by Younghee Kim-Wait, Amherst College Class of 1982. Financial support for the exhibition was provided by the Hall & Kate Peterson Fund. Finally, I would like to acknowledge Yale University Press for generously granting us copyright permission to reproduce images from Albers's *Interaction of Color* in this catalogue.

Notes

1. In February of 2014 a photograph of a dress took the Internet by storm, with some viewers arguing that it was a blue and black dress and others claiming it was white and gold. The popular coverage of this color controversy brought vision science into the forefront of popular culture. To read more about this story and its media coverage see Jonathon Mahler, "The White and Gold (No, Blue and Black!) Dress that Melted the Internet," *New York Times*, February 27, 2015.
2. Josef Albers, *Interaction of Color*, rev. ed. (1963; repr., New Haven, CT: Yale University Press, 2013).
3. Josef and Anni Albers Foundation, Josef Albers Archives, Folder 80.44 (2) III. "B. Various [The Physio-psychological phenomenon of the so called after image...]." Typescript, mimeography, undated.
4. Albers, *Interaction of Color*, 37–38.
5. For Albers's discussion of this topic, see "The Teaching of Art II: Training in Visual Experience. Interview with Mullins, Kerr, Hamilton and Albers," *Yale Reports* 54 (January 20, 1957).
6. *Life Magazine* (July 3, 1944), 39–50.
7. For more on Albers and Gestalt Theory in the Bauhaus, see Marianne L. Teuber, "Blue Night by Paul Klee," in Mary Henle, ed., *Vision and Artifact* (New York: Springer Publishing, 1976), 131–51.
8. For a discussion of Albers's interest in Gestalt psychology and its influence on his teaching, see Geert-Jan Boudewijnse, "Gestalt Theory and Bauhaus–A Correspondence between

Roy Behrens, Brenda Danilowitz, William S. Huff, Lothar Spillmann, Gerhard Stemberger and Michael Wertheimer in the Summer of 2011," *Gestalt Theory* 32:1 (2012): 81–98; and Frederick Horowitz and Brenda Danilowitz, *Josef Albers: To Open Eyes* (New York: Phaidon Press, 2009).

9. Geert-Jan Boudewijnse, "Gestalt Theory and Bauhaus," 94.

10. For instance, Albers's library contains a copy of the Pittsburgh Color Dynamics publication *Color as Light: Electromagnetic Spectrum*; a catalogue of books on color by Faber Birren, including *Monument to Color: A New Interpretation of Color Harmony Based on the Research and Findings of the Modern Psychologist* (New York: McFarlane, Warde, McFarlane, 1938). It also includes copies of vision-related books such as Bruno Peterman, *Das Gestaltproblem in Der Psychologie im Lichte analytischer Besinnung* (Leipzig: Verlag von Johann Ambrosius Barth, 1931); Nelson F. Beeler and Franklyn M. Branley, *Experiments in Optical Illusion* (New York: Thomas Y. Crowell Company, 1951); and Mathew Luckiesh, *Visual Illusions: Their Causes, Characteristics, and Applications*, introduction by William H. Ittelson (New York: Dover, 1965). Albers also corresponded with Gyorgy Kepes, founder of the MIT vision lab and author of many books that examine the interconnections of art and science. Albers's library includes many of his titles, including *Education of Vision; Structure in Art and Science* (New York: G. Braziller, 1965); *The New Landscape in Art and Science* (Chicago: Paul Theobald and Co., 1965); *The Nature and Art of Motion* (New York: G. Braziller, 1965); *Module, Proportion, Symmetry, Rhythm* (New York: G. Braziller, 1966; and *Education of Vision* (New York: G. Braziller, 1965).

11. *Yale Scientific Magazine* 40:2. (November 1965), 1–36. This issue included the following essays: Josef Albers, "Op Art and/or Perceptual Effects," 8–15; Victor Vasarely, "A New Art Through the Physical World," 16–33; Gerald Oster, "The Mind's Eye: Visions in Art and Science," 34–36.

12. John H. Holloway and John A. Weil, "A Conversation with Josef Albers," *Leonardo* 3:4 (October 1970): 460.

13. For instance, see Alan Lee, "A Critical Account of Josef Albers' Concepts of Color," *Leonardo* 14:2 (Spring 1981): 99–105. For a further discussion of this topic, see Sarah Lowengard's essay in this catalogue.

14. Charles Percy Snow, "The Two Cultures," Rede Lecture, May 7, 1959, Senate House, Cambridge University. Printed in Charles Percy Snow, *The Two Cultures* (Cambridge, U.K.: Cambridge University Press, 2001).

15. For examples, see Linda Dalrymple Henderson, *The Fourth Dimension and Non-Euclidean Geometry in Modern Art*, rev. ed. (1983; repr., Cambridge, MA: MIT Press, 2013); Gavin Parkinson, *Surrealism, Art and Modern Science: Relativity, Quantum Mechanics, Epistemology* (New Haven, CT: Yale University Press, 2008); "Art and Science: 1930–60," in Martin Hammer and Christina Lodder, eds., *Constructing Modernity: The Art and Career of Naum Gabo* (New Haven, CT: Yale University Press, 2000), 379–403; and Margaret Livingstone and David Hubel, *Vision and Art: The Biology of Seeing* (New York: Abrams, 2008).

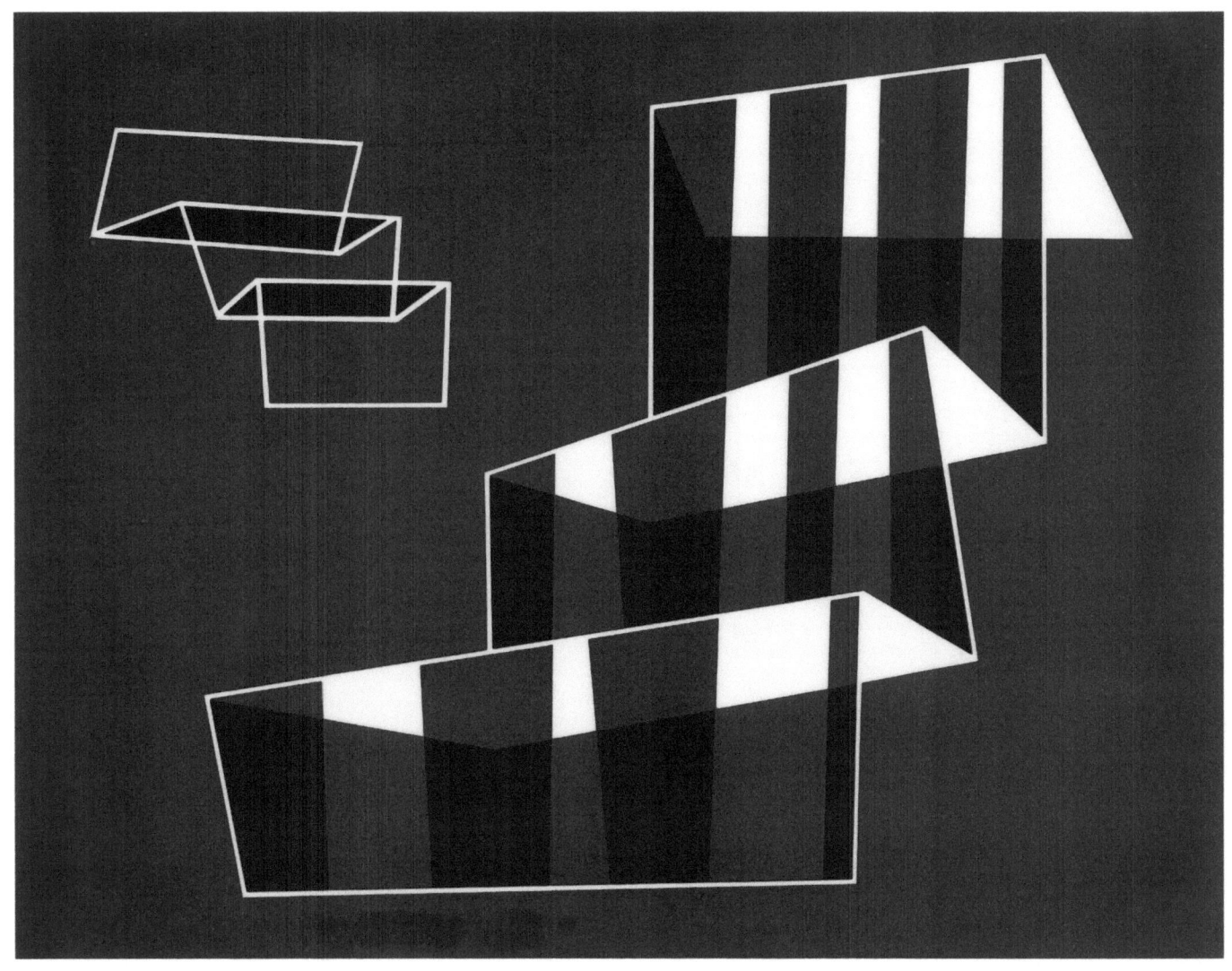

Cat. 1: Josef Albers, *Stufen* (*Steps*), 1931. Sandblasted opaque flashed glass, 16 x 21 in. (40.6 x 53.3 cm). The Josef and Anni Albers Foundation (2007.6.1).

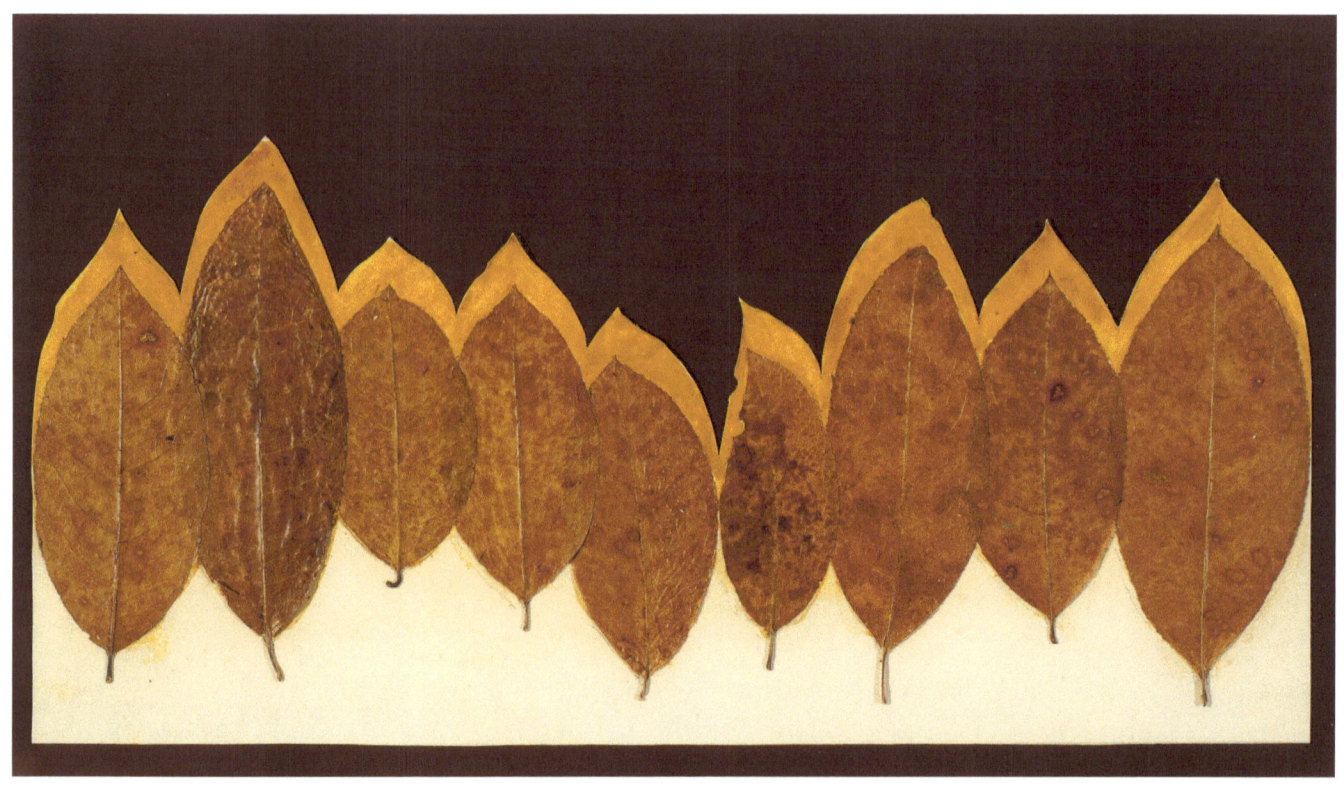

Cat. 4: Josef Albers, Leaf Study I, ca. 1940. Leaves on paper, 9 ½ x 18 in. (24.1 x 45.7 cm). The Josef and Anni Albers Foundation (1976.9.9).

A Short History of Josef Albers's *Interaction of Color*

Brenda Danilowitz

Origins: Weimar and the Bauhaus

When Josef Albers was an elementary and middle school student in Bottrop from 1895 to 1902, the young apprentices who worked for his father lived with the family in their large house on Horsterstrasse (now the site of a busy regional bus terminal). Lorenz Albers was a house painter and decorator (*Anstreichermeister*), and Josef was fond of reminiscing about the craftsmanly skills he had learned from his father.

> When asked later in life about his working methods for the [*Homage to the Square* paintings, Albers] would often explain that he always began with the center square because his father, who, among other things, painted houses, had instructed him as a young man that when you paint a door you start in the middle and work outwards. "That way you catch the drips, and don't get your cuffs dirty." [1]

It is an open question whether the senior Albers also imparted words of wisdom on the use of color to his older son. By 1905, when Josef was seventeen years old, Lorenz had risen to be deputy chairman of the Bottrop Compulsory Guild of Painters, Glass Artisans and Decorators (Maler-, Glaser- und Anstriecher-Zwangsinnung) in a fast-transforming world where artisans' guilds and associations were being overtaken by larger, more industrialized businesses.[2] Trends in house painting and decorating were also changing. As far as color was concerned, its use in nineteenth-century house interiors, like that of other consumer materials, was contingent on both fashion and economics. Pigments varied greatly in cost and quality. By the 1870s, however, "there was a reliability of nomenclature, applicability and cheapness, a wide choice of colors…and, for the home, paints that could be 'purchased ready for use' rather than mixed on site."[3] In 1852 the widely read *The Laws of Harmonious Colouring Adapted to House Painting*, written by the Scotsman David R. Hays, was published in German translation.[4] If Lorenz Albers kept up with developments in fashion and technology, it is quite possible that he may have awakened his son's fascination with color.

Once Josef Albers arrived at the Bauhaus in Weimar in 1920, he entered an environment in which matters of form in art were of primary concern. Yet of all the elements embraced by the term *form*, color is the most elusive. Color is a product both of culture and of nature, of the physics of light and the highly complicated structures of the human brain and eye. It is both absent and present, real and imagined, object and subject. Although much has been written about color teaching at the Bauhaus, Albers remembers the subject of color at the early Bauhaus as a "stepchild." "We had very little color," he remarked in a 1968 BBC interview, "real color studies, in Itten's course and in Klee's and Kandinsky's courses...."[5] Johannes Itten, an instructor, and Ludwig Hirschfeld-Mack, a fellow student, were both former students of the colorist Adolf Hölzel (1853–1934); but about Itten's color teaching Albers would later remark, "Itten thought I had no color.... I was told to go first to wallpainting because glass painting is a branch of wall painting.... I did not agree.... I had learnt wall painting in my father's workshop. I went to the wall painting workshop only to help my friends."[6]

Despite Albers's disclaimer, and although formal instruction may not have been offered, it was difficult to avoid color at the Bauhaus. Albers soon became part of a circle of established artists and architects who were all, in one way or another, investigating aspects of color in their work, including the Bauhaus founder, Walter Gropius, the painters Wassily Kandinsky, Paul Klee, and Lyonel Feininger, and younger colleagues like Oskar Schlemmer, Marcel Breuer, and Hirschfeld-Mack.[7] Color explorations at the Bauhaus during this time included the esoteric harmonizing exercises of the musician Gertrud Grunow that connected colors and musical tone through body movements; Hirschfeld-Mack's color-light-music machine; and Kandinsky's "scientific" questionnaire, which attempted to match colors, notably blue and yellow, to psychological states. The intellectual underpinnings to these studies were theories, treatises, and discourses from the late eighteenth to the early twentieth century written by scientists and philosophers including Philipp Otto Runge, Michel Eugène Chevreul, Arthur Schopenhauer, Hermann von Helmholz, and Wilhelm Ostwald.[8] Perhaps most significant was Johann Wolfgang Goethe's *Die Farbenlehre* of 1810, which became the model for Albers's color teaching.[9]

Influence of Goethe

Weimar was Goethe's adopted hometown. He moved there at age twenty-six in 1775 and remained a prominent resident until his death in 1832. Goethe's spirit must have permeated the very air of the early Bauhaus, which opened in Weimar in 1919, nearly a century after the great writer's death. Walking daily to the former Royal Reithaus in the park on the River Ilm where he gave his preliminary design course, or *Vorkurs*, from 1923 to 1925, Albers would have passed Goethe's picturesque garden house, already by 1886 a public memorial site and shrine for the writer's admirers. Goethe's writings on color were central to the teaching of Klee, who was the *Formmeister* in the weaving workshop that Anni Albers joined in 1923 and whose work and ideas were greatly admired by both Anni and Josef Albers.[10] In a 1973 letter to Rudolf Arnheim, Albers wrote, "my reading of Goethe's *Theory of Colors* goes back to a far-distant past, probably to a time before I joined the Bauhaus in 1920 when I was 32 years old...."[11]

Goethe's poetic imagination permeated Albers's teaching, especially the color course. Goethe's research in physical science never lost sight of the intimate relationship between the human being and the objects of scientific curiosity—whether physical phenomena like light or biological ones like the plants that populated his environment. Albers's insistence on the primacy of the relationships operating within a framework of known facts took its cue from Goethe, whose "course as a scientist took him not only on a search for data, but also on an active and imaginative quest for relationships in man and in nature."[12]

In his preface to *Die Farbenlehre* of 1810, translated into English as "Theory of Color," Goethe suggested a highly nuanced notion of "theory," writing that "any theoretical endeavor should do no more than outline the paths along which a deed may wander with the touch of life until it bears fruit in keeping with the laws of nature."[13] Albers's writings on color are frequently referred to, similarly, as color "theory," but Albers himself was careful to avoid that label. He always insisted that practice came before theory and that he was teaching a philosophy and a way of seeing and not a theory; we should note that Albers titled his own work *Interaction of Color*.

The part of Goethe's long and detailed treatise most relevant to Albers's enterprise is the section "Physiological Colors" at the beginning of part 1:

> It is appropriate to start with a study of physiological colors because they are wholly, or largely, a property of the observer, of the eye. These colors

> are the basis for our entire theory.... Until now, however, they have been considered inconsequential and random, an illusion and a defect. Physiological colors have been known from the earliest times, but since their fleeting quality could be neither caught nor held they were exiled to the realm of mischievous phantoms....We have called them physiological colors because they are the property of the healthy eye. We consider them innate conditions for sight, evidence of the living *interaction between its inner nature and the outer world.*[14]

Color, according to Goethe's formulation, is "a property of the observer," whose color perceptions are "fleeting." For Albers, the important distinction was between "ocular seeing," the neurobiological processes of sight, and "vision," which, coupled with imagination, is a transformative process.[15] In an undated written statement explaining the use of color in his own work, Albers gave an extended explanation of what Goethe had named "physiological colors":

> The physio-psychological phenomenon of the so-called after-image is the reason why we don't see neighboring colors as what they actually are, that is, physically.
>
> In our perception, juxtaposed colors, change each other in two ways, on the one hand in regard to light, on the other in relation to hue.
>
> As there is nothing large or small in itself but only in relationship, so any color appears lighter or darker and brighter or duller in connection with other colors.
>
> That is, a light color makes any less light one darker or heavier than it really is, and vice versa. As to hue, a strong red, for instance, pushes its neighbors towards green, its opposite hue.
>
> This effect can be understood in two ways. First as it is done usually, in an additive direction as any outspoken hue adds its complementary hue to its neighbor. But it is just as important to see this as a subtractive influence in absorbing from its neighbor its own hue, or light.
>
> This interaction of colors exists in all color combinations to a larger or smaller degree, but is in most cases unrecognizable even for trained eyes.
>
> This interaction permits the knowing colorist to make opaque colors look transparent, heavy ones turn light, colorless neutrals become colorful, warm ones seem cool, and vice versa. It makes [it] possible to make equal colors look different, and different ones look alike, that even defined shapes as well as color areas vanish from our sight.
>
> Though there are other factors which change the psychic effect of colors, as placement and shape, quantity and recurrence, in my paintings, "Homage to the Square," the interaction of color caused by juxtaposition was one of my main concerns.[16]

In the introduction to *Interaction of Color*, moreover, Albers includes a firm statement about the difference between factual "knowledge" and artistic "vision":

> The book does not begin with optics and physiology of visual perception, nor with any presentation of the physics of light and wave length.... What counts here—first and last—is not so-called knowledge of so-called facts, but vision—seeing. Seeing here implies *Schauen* (as in *Weltanschauung*) and is coupled with fantasy, with imagination.[17]

Black Mountain College and Yale University

The story of *Interaction of Color* begins late in the fall of 1933, when Josef and Anni Albers arrived in the United States. Fresh from the recently closed Bauhaus, where he had been teaching the preliminary course design, or *Vorkurs*, Josef Albers was invited to create a department of art at Black Mountain College near Asheville in rural North Carolina.

At the Bauhaus Albers had designed highly colored glass pieces (many destined for architectural installation) as well as furniture, wallpaper, and a typeface. In 1928 he acquired a Leica camera and immersed himself in photography. Design and photography would remain professional interests, and he would continue to teach a version of the *Vorkurs*, which at Black Mountain was called *Werklehre* and was described in the college catalogue as teaching "the development of the feeling for material and space."[18] At Yale, from 1950 on, the course morphed into "Basic Design."

At Black Mountain College Albers resumed the practice of painting he had put aside during his Bauhaus years, and it was also at Black Mountain that he launched the first color course in an American art school curriculum. He initially relied on conventional methods to introduce color to his students: the color wheels and systems of Goethe, Schopenhauer, and Ostwald (fig. 5). But he soon moved away from that approach, encouraging students to understand color by creating their own color studies based on a series of exercises that led them to discern the differences in hues, tones, and intensity, not as definitions and diagrams to be learned by rote, but by comparison and through trial-and-error experience. It was a way of teaching color that was Albers's own and at Black Mountain College it took

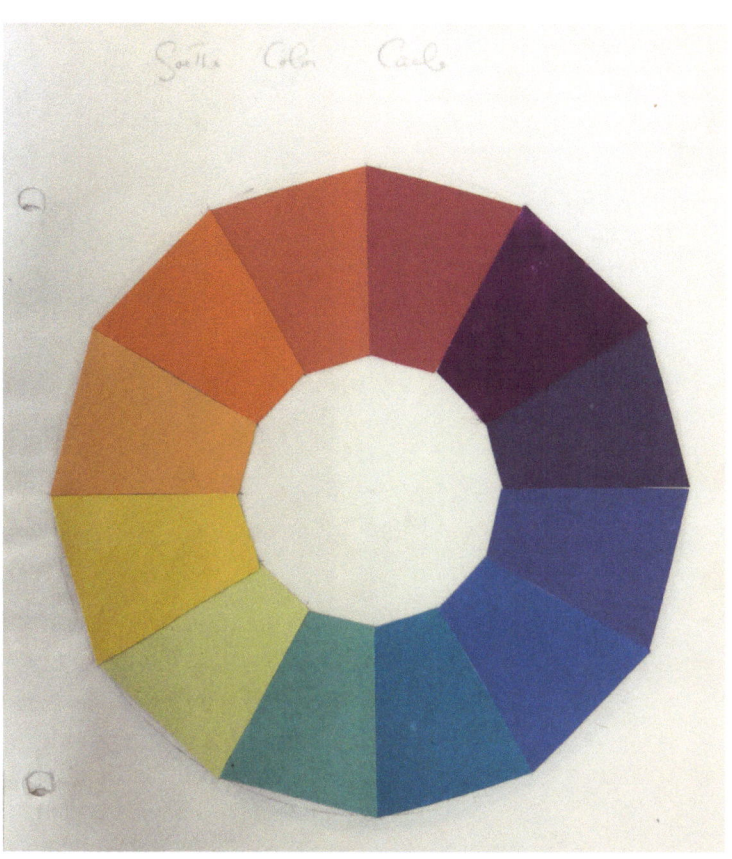

Figure 5: Barbara (Bobbie) Dreier, Goethe Color Circle. Cut and pasted paper on a page from a notebook from Josef Albers's color class, Black Mountain College, 1935. The Theodore and Barbara Loines Dreier Black Mountain College Collection, State Archives of North Carolina, Western Regional Archives, Asheville, NC (PC 1956.17).

Figure 6: Josef Albers teaching the color class, Black Mountain College, summer 1944. Photo: Josef Breitenbach. Courtesy the Breitenbach Trust, New York, and the Josef and Anni Albers Foundation.

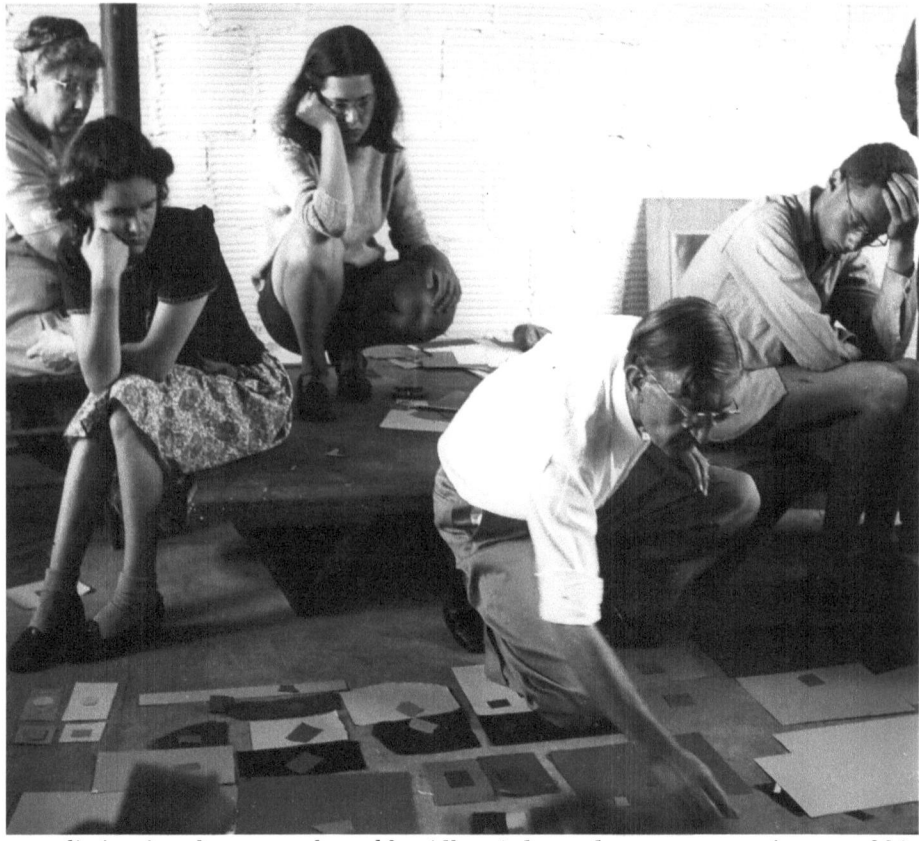

on a distinctive character, shaped by Albers's long classroom experience and his insistence on hands-on learning.

The best way to appreciate what was so unusual about Albers's way of teaching is to examine photographs of him in action in the classroom (fig. 6). He was constantly in motion, getting up close to his students, subtly in command, guiding and nudging them. In photographs from Black Mountain Albers is seen sitting among his students, getting down on the floor, putting himself on their level. The photos convey activity and vitality. Photographers who visited the college—among them Josef Breitenbach (1896-1984), Genevieve Naylor (1915-1989), and Clemens Kalischer (b.1921)—captured multiple images of Albers in action. Later at Yale, in 1954, Albers's student John Cohen made a series of photographs and a short 16mm movie in Albers's classroom. As a consummate performer, Albers seemed not to consider the photographers' presence an intrusion. The sight of him teaching was so compelling that it may have made him the most photographed teacher in history.

For Albers, teaching and learning were not a matter of the teacher imparting privileged information and the student acquiring received knowledge. Teaching involved asking questions, not providing answers; and Albers always privileged learning over teaching. His idea of education—true to its Latin root *e-ducere*, to lead or to lead out—was to draw out the creativity that is part of being human. "Art is a demonstration of human life," he said. "Art is revelation instead of information."[19]

The notion that we learn best by direct experience is a familiar one, expressing an ideal state of education. But while it is often touted, it is seldom followed. Albers was one of the few who could make "learning by doing" a reality. His methods were direct, consistent, and free of cant. Practice, doing, trying, experimenting, playing—all of these concepts were brought to life in his classes. Theory, rules, dates, and information were secondary and would come later. For Albers true learning was a physical and a collective act. It led to insight, vision, and imagination. It took courage, and gave confidence in return.

Albers's holistic view of the world and of life led to his classroom focus on context, contiguity, and relationships among elements as the key to understanding both the real world and the world the artist creates. Of all the elements of art—shape, space, color, texture, and so on—color, to Albers, was "the most relative medium."[20] Color relationships were the most powerfully demonstrable and decisive; "*how* a color is used and related to others...is decisive in art."[21]

In Albers's color class there were few materials and they seldom varied: colored paper swatches, rubber cement, cutting tools (scissors, knives, razor blades), cutting boards, and cardboard for mounting the completed studies. He would present the exercise in few words, then circulate among the students observing their work, sometimes sitting down beside a student, making certain his charges understood the task. "Albers," wrote one student, "is interested in what is happening out there where the colors are actually interacting: the objectivity, the dedicated accuracy of observation, the sheer hard work he requires, amount to a selflessness unseen in the art world since the Middle Ages."[22]

The goal of the exercises was not to elicit a single correct answer but to engage students in active experimentation that would yield many and varying solutions—that would extend the question or investigation at hand and suggest new ones: to get them to "see color action as well as feel color relatedness."[23] Conveying his accumulated experience of how colors behaved and how color relationships worked was the point of the class; guiding the students' own first exploratory steps in gaining their own experience was the means by which it was accomplished.

The Publication of *Interaction of Color*

In January 1928 Albers had written from the Bauhaus to his friends Franz and Friedel Perdekamp, "This year I am turning 40. Therefore I have to be successful soon. Two things I am planning for this year: a pedagogical book about my teaching...and an exhibition of my new glass pictures."[24] The unrealized book was to have been one in the now legendary series of "Bauhaus Books" (*Bauhausbücher*).[25] As it turned out, three-and-a-half decades would pass before a book on Albers's teaching was realized.

The idea of publishing a volume about Albers's color course came under discussion at Yale University Press in 1956. The initial response, according to the press's deputy director, Howard Sayre Weaver, was that such a project was "quite out of the question." To reproduce the Albers color course the book would need to cover an extensive area, convey Albers's idiosyncratic and poetic "voice," and be simultaneously academic and anti-academic—placing practice before theory (an Albers absolute). "Above all," Weaver said, "it would have to contain color embodying a degree of precision not ordinarily necessary in books of any kind. It would have to be not a book *about* color but nothing less than a book *of* color." Four-color printing was not capable of reproducing the studies from Albers's class with the necessary specificity, purity, and opacity of color. "Even if a means could be found," Weaver said, "the project would be so elaborate and costly that no publisher could reasonably be expected to take it seriously."[26]

But Albers, charismatic, authoritative, and contagiously enthusiastic, had a dedicated following of true believers, and with Yale University Press eventually taking the lead, an unprecedented and original collaboration began. While the press was securing funding (an estimated $35,000–$50,000), work on the text, the design, and production began.

Albers had little if any experience with the screen-printing process before 1956, when two former students—Sewell Sillman, Albers's hands-on teaching assistant in the color course, and the graphic designer Norman Ives—were enlisted to oversee design and production of the catalogue of a retrospective exhibition of Albers's work at the Yale University Art Gallery. Albers was especially eager to have his *Homage to the Square* paintings reproduced in a way that would come as close as possible to replicating their powerful demonstrations of color interaction. Sillman experimented with screen printing, and the first *Homage to the Square* screenprints were born as two tipped-in plates in the catalogue (fig

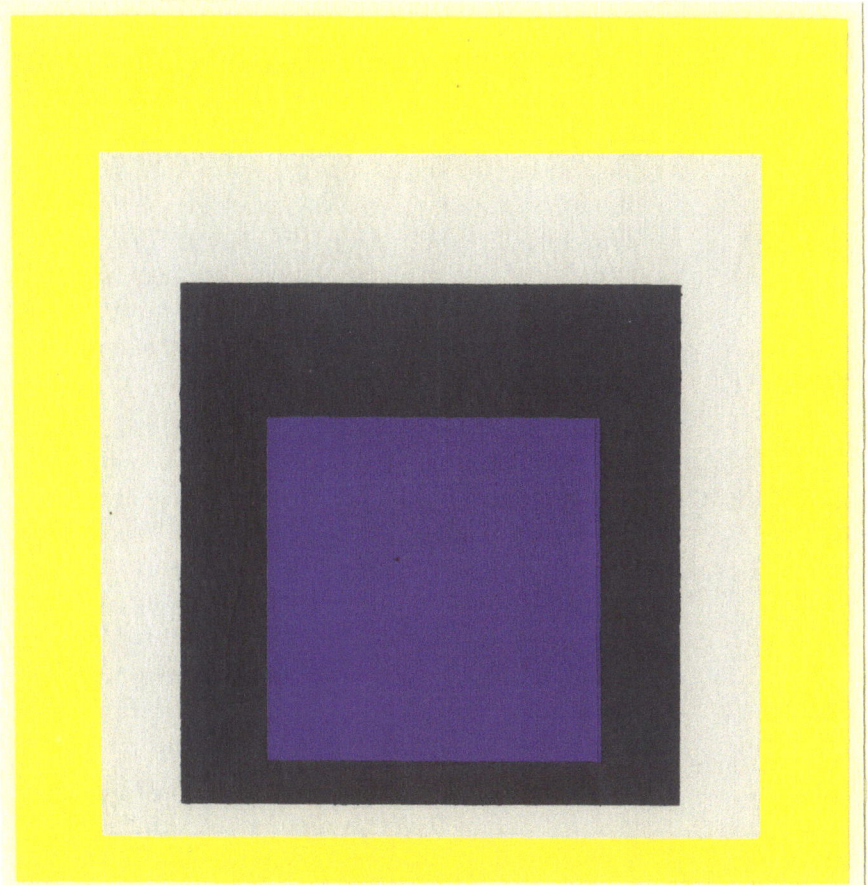

Figure 7: Screenprint of Josef Albers, *Homage to the Square: Dedicated*, 1955. Oil on Masonite, 43 x 43 in. (109.2 x 109.2 cm). Collection of the Albright-Knox Art Gallery, Buffalo, NY. This screenprint was pasted in as the frontispiece to the catalogue of the exhibition Josef Albers: Paintings Prints Projects at the Yale University Art Gallery, April 25–June 18, 1956.

7). It was a watershed moment in Albers's career and would enable not only the production of *Interaction of Color* but also an array of screen-printed editions of his work that continued for the next twenty years—the remainder of his life.

Working closely with Albers, Sillman mixed an astonishing eight-hundred–plus colored inks for the plates of *Interaction of Color* while Ives came up with a three-part design for the publication: a volume referred to as "Text"; eighty individual folders containing the color studies (for the most part accurate re-creations of works made of colored paper by students in the color course); and a companion volume titled "Commentary"—Albers's directions to readers and his discussion of individual plates. Albers specified an arrangement and typography that paralleled the rhythms and cadences of his speech, and he wrote the entire text.

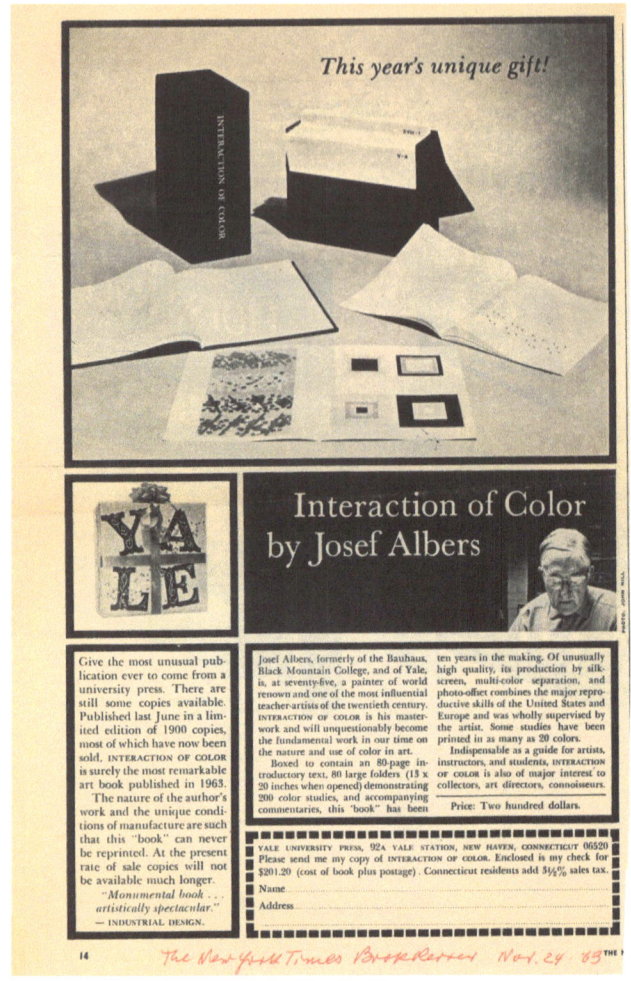

Figure 8: Advertisement for *Interaction of Color*, *New York Times Book Review*, November 24, 1963, 14.

Sixteen of the folders were simply unsuited to screenprinting and were completed by a combination of four-color letterpress and offset lithography. The letterpress plates were made in the Netherlands by the firm Enschedé, of Haarlem, and Connecticut Printers Inc. did the printing. The offset lithography as well as the printing of the "Text" and "Commentary" were the work of Yale University Press's own Carl Purington Rollins, longtime manager of the manufacturing department at Yale University Press and Printer to the University at Yale. Apart from the letterpress plates, therefore, *Interaction of Color* was made entirely in the U.S.

Because of the huge scale of the project, the screenprinting was divided among three separate companies—R. H. Norton and Company and Sirocco Screenprints in New Haven, and Homer Mitchell in Detroit. Proofing of the sixty-four screenprinted folders (120 studies) was exacting and arduous—a perfect analogue of the attention and craftsmanship Albers demanded of his students. Albers was closely involved and in several cases wrote the final commentary only after approving its related color study so that the two elements would be matched precisely.

Collating and assembling the two thousand three-part volumes and the folders was no less of a challenge. Weaver recounted how the one hundred and sixty thousand individual folders arrived at the Yale Press offices in wooden boxes specially constructed to avoid compression and possible damage to the printed surfaces. Each folder was inspected, folded, interleaved with a slip-sheet, and manually inserted into its portfolio box together with a "Commentary" volume. Finally the portfolio box and the "Text" volume were inserted into a slipcase and boxed.

Yale Art School students were engaged to help assemble the folders. For some it was their first encounter with the Albers color course, which, although it continued to be a course option taught by other instructors, was by 1963 already losing the master's imprint.

The Reception of *Interaction of Color*

When *Interaction of Color* was released to the public in 1963, Yale University Press promoted its unconventional format, its "un-bookness" (fig. 8). Reporters in daily newspapers dutifully recounted the book's vital statistics, and especially its high price. Reviewers in professional journals cited Albers's mastery of color, articulated in the book, as a reason that his practices were distinct from the apparently arbitrary use of color associated with the rising group of "color field" painters. Critics like Nancy Malone, who had some experience of Albers's teaching, pointed out the complexity of *Interaction of Color*. Malone advised her readers to have "a comfortable chair, a large table, and a good bit of time" to come to grips with this "very large book [which] cannot be assimilated quickly. In fact," she continued "any attempt to comprehend it at one sitting or skim it for its flavor, is guaranteed to result in visual dazzlement and intellectual bewilderment.... Begin slowly."[27] Howard Sayre Weaver cautioned, "Before it will be truly rewarding, *Interaction of Color*—like Josef Albers himself—will be demanding. It is to be looked *through* and used, as a sort of grand passport to perception."[28]

By the beginning of 1968 *Interaction of Color* had sold out. Most of the two thousand copies had gone to museums and collectors or to schools and libraries, where they were invariably treated as precious objects. In many places, if students were allowed to consult them at all they were required to wear white gloves and submit to the vigilant supervision of an instructor or librarian.[29]

Although complete German (1972) and Finnish (1978) editions of *Interaction of Color* were published subsequently, these did not satisfy the demand for the book from the English-speaking world, and so in 1971 Albers adapted it into a smaller pocket edition for Yale University Press (reprinted in 1974). This edition and later paperback versions reproduced the entire original text but with only ten color plates. The book was used frequently as a textbook in schools, where students often had access to the original publication in their libraries, and sales soared. Editions in Japanese, French, Spanish, Swedish, and Italian followed German and Finnish paperback editions. With the exception of the Japanese and Swedish editions, all remain in print. The paperback has been revised and expanded and currently contains many more color plates than the original one. Portuguese, Korean, basic (or simplified) Chinese, Hungarian, and Norwegian editions have been added. With the publication in 2014 of Estonian

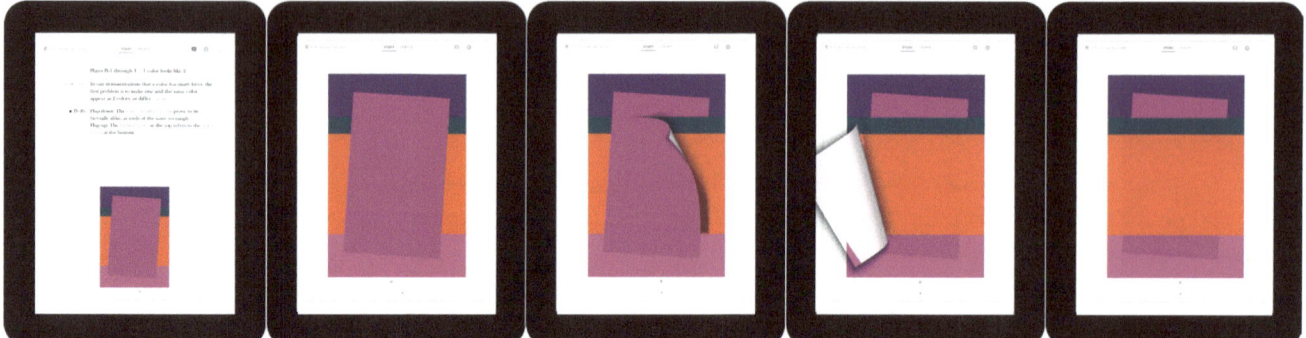

Figure 9: Screenshots showing the interactive Plate IV-4 from the digital iPad App of Josef Albers, *Interaction of Color*, iPad ver. 1.5 (New Haven: Yale University Press, 2014). Image courtesy the Josef and Anni Albers Foundation/Yale University Press.

and, in 2015, a complex (or traditional) Chinese paperback edition, *Interaction of Color* continues to find new audiences.

Close to a half million paperback copies of *Interaction of Color* have been sold worldwide since 1971, and demand shows no signs of slowing. In 2009 Yale University Press published a deluxe two-volume "New Complete" edition—one volume containing the original "Text" and "Commentary," the other containing all the original plates reproduced by a four-color digital process. Most of the students, artists, designers, architects, and members of the general public who now buy and study *Interaction of Color* do so without ever having seen the original edition or having the screen-printed color plates to guide them. Many are unaware of the existence of the 1963 portfolio.

The App

In 1994, after several years of development, Yale University Press, in collaboration with the Josef and Anni Albers Foundation, published an electronic version of *Interaction of Color* with software available on floppy disk and CD-ROM. Although for its time this was a groundbreaking effort, it was problematic. The program was clunky and cumbersome; it was created for the Macintosh computer—the only hardware that could support such an effort—at a time when very few people besides graphic designers used Macs; and technology was changing so rapidly that the cost of updating the software was financially unsustainable. Though welcomed by teachers of color courses and their students, it was technically and economically unviable.

As a result, in 2010 the publishers of *Interaction of Color* decided that the fiftieth anniversary of the original edition, 2013, was the perfect time to reincarnate Albers's now classic masterwork in digital form. With a concerted effort and substantial investment the new App was born, taking advantage of all the capabilities of the latest technology.[30] Seamlessly woven into the App is an introduction with a video of Albers, short video explanations of some of the more complicated studies, and testimonial videos by artists, architects, and designers. Text and plates run side by side so that the commentaries are easily integrated into the viewing experience. There is also a complete section titled "Create" in which users can select from five hundred and twenty-six colors to create, save, and share their own studies. The beauty of this new *Interaction of Color* is the elegance with which all the parts of the original have been layered, with no loss of design or content. Retaining Albers's design had been an absolute requirement, and the developers embraced the challenge in true Albersian spirit.

Conclusion

The idea at the core of Albers's educational philosophy, that learning is a collective and social process, is enshrined in *Interaction of Color*. It is expressed from the very beginning in Albers's dedication of the book to his students and in his acknowledgement of their role as the original creators of the color studies. Nevertheless, the belief persists that *Interaction of Color* is a book about Albers's color "theory" and that the color plates serve as demonstrations of that presumed theory.

But *Interaction of Color* is not a theory, a treatise on color, a textbook, or a teaching manual. It is the demonstration of a method of sharpening the eye toward increased color perception and discrimination so that readers will come to a nuanced understanding of how color behaves. In Albers's own words, it is simply "a record of an experimental way of studying color and of teaching color."[31]

Notes

1. Nicholas Fox Weber, "The Artist as Alchemist," in *Josef Albers: A Retrospective* (New York: Harry N. Abrams, Inc. and Solomon R. Guggenheim Museum, 1988), 15. For more on Josef Albers's early life, see Brenda Danilowitz, "Teaching Design: A Short History of Josef Albers," in Frederick A. Horowitz and Brenda Danilowitz, *Josef Albers: To Open Eyes: The Bauhaus, Black Mountain and Yale* (New York: Phaidon Press, 2006), 9–10.
2. Johannes Geurts, ed., *Funfzig Jahre Malerinnung Bottrop* (Bottrop: W. Postberg, 1955). My thanks to Charles Darwent for pointing out this source.
3. Stefan Muthesius, *The Poetic Home: Designing the 19th-Century Domestic Interior* (New York: Thames & Hudson, 2009), 124.
4. David Ramsey Hay, *The Laws of Harmonious Colouring: Adapted to House Painting* (Edinburgh: D. Lizars, 1828); translated by L. Huettmann as *Die Gesetze der Farbenharmonie vorzüglich für die Zwecke der Haus-, Studen- und Decorationsmalerei* (Weimar: B. F.Voigt, 1852).

5. BBC interview, June 20, 1968, cited in Frederick A. Horowitz, "The Color Course," in Horowitz and Danilowitz, 269 n. 19. A full audiotape of BBC interview is available in the Josef and Anni Albers Foundation archive of audiovisual materials. For a detailed discussion of Albers's experience as a student at the early Bauhaus, see Brenda Danilowitz, "Teaching Design: A Short History of Josef Albers," in Horowitz and Danilowitz, 16–20.

6. Josef Albers, interviewed by Irving L. Finkelstein, January 2, 1966, Yale University Library Historical Sound Recordings. Digital copy in the Josef and Anni Albers Foundation archive of audio-visual materials.

7. Albers, who had quickly risen from being a student to the position of *Geselle*, or journeyman, in Weimar, was made a *Jungmeister* (junior master) when the Bauhaus moved to Dessau in 1925. See Danilowitz, "Teaching Design," 25. Although Hirschfeld-Mack, a former student, was not officially a Bauhaus master, it was he who gave the first, and unofficial, color course at the Bauhaus in Weimar in the winter semester of 1922–23. See Rainer K. Wick, *Teaching at the Bauhaus* (Hatje-Cantz: Ostfildern, 2000), 113, cited in Andrew McNamara, "The Colour of Modernism: Colour-Form Experiments in Europe and Australia," in *Europa! Europa? The Avant-Garde, Modernism and the Fate of a Continent*, ed. Sascha Bru et al. (Berlin: Walter de Gruyter, 2009), 502.

8. Philipp Otto Runge (1777–1810), *Die Farben-kugel* (Hamburg: Perthes, 1810); Michel Eugène Chevreul (1786–1889), *De la loi du contraste simultané des couleurs et de l'assortiment des objets colorés* (Paris: Pitois-Levrault, 1839); Arthur Schopenhauer (1788–1860), *Über das Sehn und die Farben: Eine Abhandlund* (Leipzig: F. A. Brockhaus, 1816); Hermann von Helmholz (1821–1894), *Über Goethes naturwissenschaftliche Arbeiten: Vortrag gehalten in der Deutschen Gesellschaft zu Königsberg* (Braunschweig: Friedrich Vieweg & Sohn, 1865); Wilhelm Ostwald (1853–1932), *Die Farbenfibel* (Leipzig: Verlag Unesma, 1917). Ostwald gave a series of lectures at the Bauhaus in Dessau in 1927.

9. For a more detailed discussion of color systems and theorists of this period and their relevance to Albers, see Horowitz and Danilowitz, *Josef Albers*, 195–97.

10. See Jenny Anger, "Anni Albers's Thank You to Paul Klee," in Brenda Danilowitz and Heinz Liesbrock, eds., *Anni and Josef Albers: Latin American Journeys* (Hatje-Cantz: Ostfildern, 2007), 159–63. For Klee's teaching and its dependence on Goethe, see Fabienne Eggelhöffer and Marianne Keller Tschirren, "Bildnerische Gestaltungslehre: Teaching Pictorial Form" and Keller Tschirren, "Color," in *Paul Klee: Bauhaus Master*, Catalogue of an exhibition at Fundación Juan March, Madrid, March 22–June 30, 2013 (Madrid: Fundación Juan March, 2013).

11. Josef Albers to Rudolf Arnheim, March 14, 1973, cited in Rudolf Arnheim, "A Critical Account of Some of Joseph [*sic*] Albers' Concepts of Color," in *Leonardo* 15:2 (1982): 174–76. My thanks to Anthony Oates for referring me to this article.

12. Douglas E. Miller, "Goethe's Color Studies in a New Perspective: *Die Farbenlehre* in English," in *Goethe and the Sciences: A Reappraisal*, ed. Frederick Amrine, Francis J. Zucker, and Harvey Wheeler (Dordrecht: D. Reidel 1987), 102.

13. Johann Wolfgang Goethe, *Goethe: The Collected Works Volume 12, Scientific Studies*, ed. and trans. Douglas E. Miller (Princeton: Princeton University Press, 1995), 168–69.

14. Goethe, *Scientific Studies*, 168 (emphasis added).

15. Josef Albers, *Search Versus Re-Search* (Hartford, CT: Trinity College Press, 1969), 17.

16. Josef and Anni Albers Foundation archive, Josef Albers Papers Box 80, Folder 44 (2).

17. Josef Albers, *Interaction of Color* (New Haven: Yale University Press, 1963), 11. Douglas Miller translates Goethe's *Anschauen* as "intuitive perception" ("Goethe's Color Studies," 107). Like Goethe, Albers uses *Schauen* and *Weltanschauen*, not simply as "looking" or "seeing" but with the added meaning he intends with the word "vision."
18. "Black Mountain College 1935–1936," Black Mountain College Museum + Arts Center Collection, D. H. Ramsey Library Special Collections, University of North Carolina–Asheville, http://toto.lib.unca.edu/findingaids/mss/bmcmac/01_bmcmac_publications/bmcmac_pub_03_1935-36/default_bmcmac_pub_1935-36.htm, accessed June 23, 2015.
19. Josef Albers, "On the Meaning of Art," paper presented at Berea College, Berea, Kentucky, March 12, 1940, and at Black Mountain College, May 6, 1940. Typescript in the Josef and Anni Albers Foundation archive, Josef Albers Papers, Series IIa: Box 39, Folder 26.
20. Albers, *Interaction of Color*, 10. This line invariably appears, usually on the first page, of surviving notebooks of students in Albers's color course.
21. Albers, "On the Meaning of Art."
22. Nancy Malone, "Albers on Color," *Industrial Design* 10 (September 1963), 68.
23. Albers, *Interaction of Color*, 10.
24. Josef Albers to Franz and Friedel Perdekamp, January 1, 1928. Private Collection, Recklinghausen, copy at the Josef and Anni Albers Foundation.
25. The proposed title, "J. Albers: Funktionsformen," was among 31 titles listed as "in preparation" in Kandinsky's *Punkt und Linie zu Flache* (Point and Line to Plane), published as *Bauhaus Book 9* in 1926. All 31 remained unpublished. See Adrian Sudhalter, "Walter Gropius and Lazlo Moholy-Nagy Bauhaus Book Series, 1925–1930," in *Bauhaus 1919–1933: Workshops for Modernity*, ed. Barry Bergdoll and Leah Dickerman (New York: The Museum of Modern Art, 2009) fn. 9, 199. My thanks to Jeannette Redensek for this information and reference.
26. Howard Sayre Weaver, "Seeing Color," *Collector's Quarterly Report* (1963), 26.
27. Malone, "Albers on Color," 67.
28. Weaver, "Seeing Color," 28.
29. The information in this and the following section is based on the author's own experience while collaborating with Yale University Press and from conversations with staff members of the Yale University Press.
30. For information on the App developed for the Apple iPad, see the iTunes Store or http://yupnet.org/interactionofcolor/.
31. Albers, *Interaction of Color*, 10.

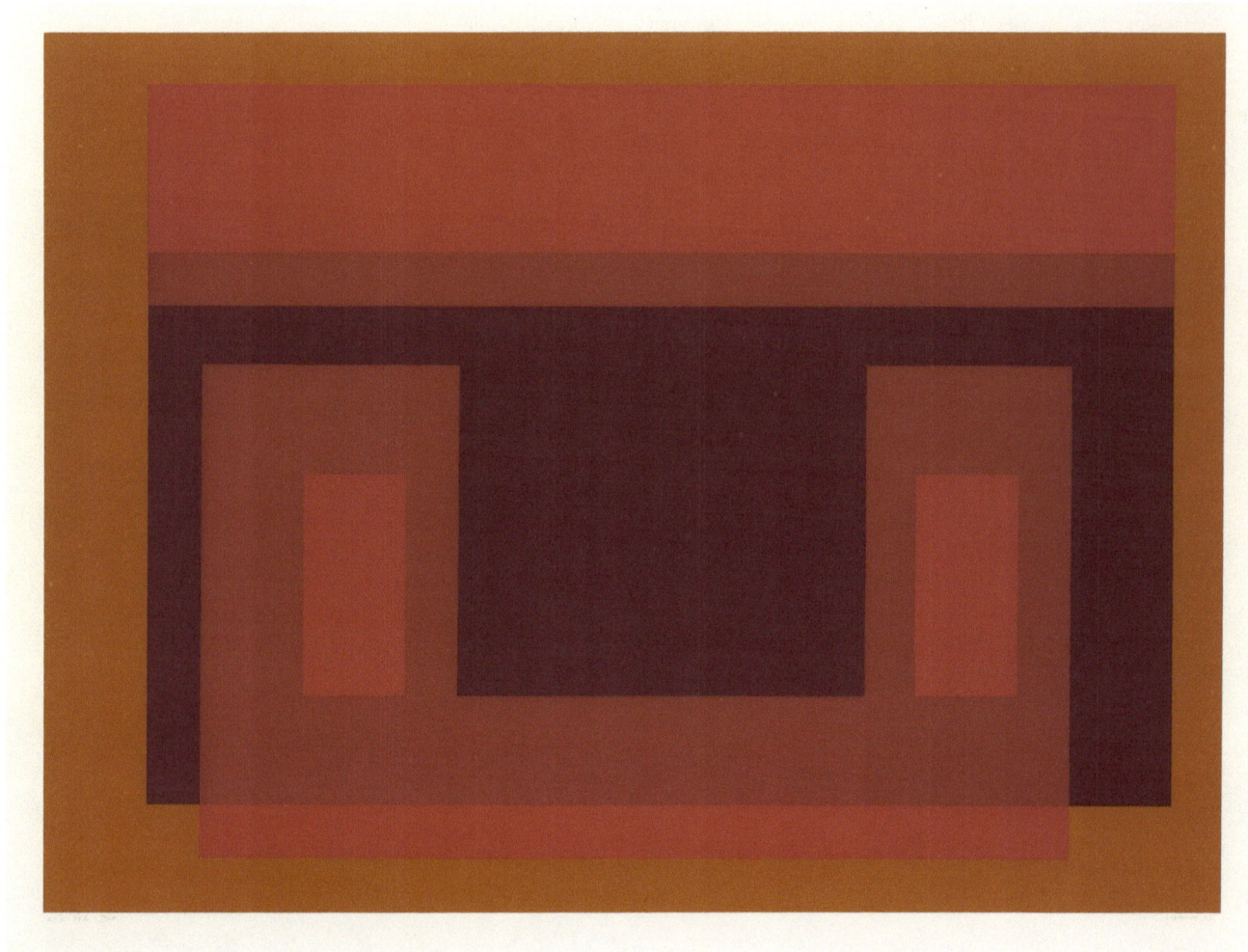

Cat. 8: Josef Albers, *I-S Va 2*, 1969. Screenprint on Arches paper, 28 x 36 in. (71.1 x 91.4 cm). Mead Art Museum, Amherst College, gift of William W. Collins, Class of 1953, in Memory of Wortham Collins (1975.103).

Explaining Color in Two 1963 Publications

Sarah Lowengard

Introduction

Modern descriptions of both science and art, especially those of the twentieth-century West, often presume an underlying opposition or indifference between the two as areas of endeavor and inquiry; it is the rare artist who engages in a substantive way with science, and an unusual scientist who is dedicated to creating art in her or his work. Practitioners of either the sciences or the arts today may consider this dichotomy nonsense, a concept closely tied to the heroic view of practitioners of both disciplines. Nevertheless, an enormous body of literature, especially but not exclusively that written for a popular audience, identifies and supports assumptions that the two realms have fundamentally different and incompatible natures. According to this point of view, the "arts" are cultural and personal expressions, while the "sciences," rooted in the verifiable, are impartial and impersonal. By extension, artists' practices are largely intuitive—even when they claim to be logical—while those of scientists are inherently rational, even if the result is aesthetically pleasing.

Thus we expect artistic descriptions that are also scientific to be unusual, and scientific descriptions to be inartistic in their essence. Advocates for the extreme form of this dichotomy may point to the historical opposition between the mathematical explanations of color offered by Sir Isaac Newton (1643–1727) and published as *Opticks* in 1704, versus those of romantic philosopher Johann Wolfgang von Goethe (1749–1832) in his multi-volume *Farbenlehre* (*Theory of Colors*, which appeared between 1791 and 1807). Indeed, Goethe's insistence on the irrelevance of Newtonian mathematics to what he considered a useful or worldly understanding of color has sometimes served as a marker of antiscientific approaches to the expansion of knowledge.[1]

What about the study of color, however? Color is an unavoidable phenomenon in both worlds. In science as in art, it defines and differentiates; it secures meanings and significances. Color is complicated to produce and reproduce but familiar to specialists and nonspecialists alike. Its long and tangled history is not controlled by either sciences or arts. Artistic descriptions must engage, at least on some level, with the quantified thought associated with scientific understanding. Any scientific uses of color must acknowledge the constraints involved in the interpretation of color information.

In this essay I examine some mid-twentieth century conflicts and connections between the worlds of art and science through a consideration of two approaches to teaching and learning about color. The monumental *Interaction of Color* (1963) by the artist Josef Albers is a systematic and nonacademic tool designed to guide art students in the use of color.[2] The physically smaller but comparably important *Color: A Guide to Basic Facts and Concepts*, also published in 1963, was issued under the aegis of the Inter-Society Color Council (ISCC), a professional society of color scientists devoted to exploring the broadly interdisciplinary nature of color.[3] The books share two explicit goals: to engage students in learning about color and to serve as an ongoing reference for future work. They have, however, different audiences in view: Albers taught, and was writing to, students who aspired to be artists, while the ISCC's constituency and primary audience was students of color sciences and their instructors—scientists or engineers. The underlying assumption of both works is that a thorough understanding of color phenomena will expand the techniques available to the student and lead to improved results, whether in the coloring of objects, the analysis of color in objects, or the creation of works of art. The authors of both books responded to a perceived lack of systematic studies of color, but the published results are vastly different. These differences highlight—if inadvertently—broader public expectations about the differences between art and science.

Other than the serendipity of a common publication year, these books have only one, tenuous link: a 1964 review of *Interaction of Color* published by one coauthor of the ISCC publication in the *ISCC Newsletter*.[4] Albers published nothing comparable or reciprocal that might illuminate the contemporary artist's view of the sciences, and there is no way to identify, for example, a possible overlap in terms of the books' audience or influence, or other issues common to studies of the reception and diffusion of intellectual and practical ideas. Nevertheless, an examination of these works together, along with the ISCC review, contributes to our understanding of mid-twentieth-century attitudes toward both science and art, their connections or disconnections. Such an examination, in turn, helps us analyze and understand approaches to these same issues now, more than fifty years later.

The Books and Their Authors

In this volume and elsewhere, Brenda Danilowitz describes the history and circumstances of Albers's inspiration and teaching and the ways they led to the publication of *Interaction of Color*.[5] Albers's course on color, offered at Black Mountain College and at Yale, provided art students with a regularized and reproducible approach to a subject that had no established place in the art history curriculum and was taught differently (or, as Albers might have said, indifferently) within each art program.[6] He emphasized the need for a thorough knowledge of color by all artists. "In visual perception a color is almost never seen as it really is—as it physically is," he said. "This fact makes color the most relative medium in art."[7] Vision cannot be wholly separated from context, and context cannot always be controlled. Therefore, Albers taught his students that an artist's studies and training must go beyond strictly aesthetic notions of connoisseurship and the artist's "eye," acknowledging the ways in which psychology and physiology influence individual perception.

Interaction of Color was the culmination of Albers's own observations about color and his experiences teaching color to art students. Published after his retirement from Yale, the book is simultaneously a memoir of his teaching experiences and an instruction book for students of art and design. A student who uses the publication as a textbook is led from basic ideas about color memory and relationships, through exercises to understand relationships between materials and color, into more advanced and self-directed ideas about color and practices that encourage "seeing what happens between colors."[8]

Color: A Guide to Basic Facts and Concepts was published by the ISCC as a response to common concerns within industry, manufacturing, engineering, and elsewhere about the need for standardization of terminology, color specification, and color measurement. The ISCC is a consortium of scientific and professional societies, standards organizations, and individuals interested in scientific and technological aspects of color.[9] Established in 1931 to coordinate and disseminate information about color across scientific disciplines, it included such founding members as the Optical Society of America, the Illuminating Engineering Association, the U.S. Pharmacopoeia Convention, and the American Association of Textile Chemists and Colorists. While individuals were also welcomed as members, the early mission of the ISCC was to identify and address the common needs of constituent professional organizations, particularly problems related to color management. Directors and committee members for the ISCC were mostly physicists and psychologists, although concerns about art training were evident among the early participants and in the earliest programs.[10]

The ISCC was aware of the problems of color in art education and, in 1942 and 1947, sponsored meetings about that topic. One active member in the first years was Royal B. Farnham, executive vice-president of the Rhode Island School of Design; representatives from such art organizations as the National Academy of Design, the National Federated Council on Art Education, and the National Alliance of Art and Industry were welcomed at meetings, although none of these groups was a formal member in those early days.[11]

A foundational project of the ISCC was the creation of descriptive standards for the color sciences that would remain viable across materials, outcomes, and languages. In 1956, the Problems Committee, the group that oversaw the standards process, approved plans to consider "the basic principles which should be included in any elementary teaching of color."[12] The report of this ISCC subcommittee (the "Subcommittee for Problem 20: Basic Elements of Color Education," the body charged with the specific task of standards for color education) was *Color: A Guide to Basic Facts and Concepts*, first published in 1963.

In the preface to the *Guide* the authors describe their charge as addressing the need for a document that defines standards as a common reference for color scientists. It would be a handbook, but not necessarily an introductory text. The authors emphasize its value as a tool for collaboration, freeing its users from the need to identify and answer basic questions; it would thus facilitate conversations across specialties. In the introduction ("The Concept of Color"), they acknowledge the problems inherent in their task, given that "the concepts represented by the word 'color' are and have been many and varied."[13] This statement echoes Albers's comments about the relativity of color, but members of the subcommittee indicated a different kind of engagement with the issue. They describe the characteristics of any color as a function of energy and reflectance (or transmittance), tempered to some degree by the observer's memory of similar objects, the surround, the adaptive state of the observer, neighboring objects, and the observer's attitude at the moment. For the purposes of the *Guide* the authors limited their discussion of color to its role as "an aspect of visual experience that may be referred to by scales of hue, saturation, and brightness, comprising a three-dimensional complex apart from spatial and temporal aspects of visual experience."[14] This is a valuable description, one with meaning to art students or artists as well as scientists concerned with color phenomena. At the same time, the "apart from" caveat makes clear the limited relevance, seen from the perspective of the *Guide*'s authors, of subjectivity. It highlights the authors' quest for a scientific foundation for descriptions of visual experience very different from Albers's notion of the relativity of color.

Like *Interaction of Color*, the *Guide* builds from the basic details of color to more complicated ones. It is organized into three sections representing graduated levels of knowledge. In the first part, the authors present such basic facts as definitions of color and the nature of normal color response. The second section considers applied facts, including color-stimulus measurement and color names as a form of color specification. The final part presents facts deemed "marginal" to the goals of the subcommittee but still important, such as theories of color vision and experimental color aesthetics. Each portion is organized, as in any technical document, according to a numbered outline and gives a unique identifier for each statement. The structure simplifies the task of locating the specifics of any topic, identifying further reading (the book includes a bibliography of about 300 entries), and incorporating its information into ongoing research or reports.

Thus *Color: A Guide to the Basic Facts and Concepts* offers color scientists a system to understand and describe what color is and how to calculate its behavior. In terms of this general goal, the book is not so different from Albers's work. What *is* different is the concern by the authors of the *Guide* for verified or quantifiable facts about color, and for creating a formal nomenclature. This would counter reliance on subjective matters of perception or taste, for which, as they noted, there could be no scientific consensus.

The crucial concern of the ISCC subcommittee, and indeed of most undertakings by the ISCC in its early years, was the definition and confirmation of empirical information about color. Any viable definition of "color" had to be represented by a set of replicable operations performed in a laboratory and interpreted through mathematics. Variables such as observer memory and attitude or the context of a color's presentation—while acknowledged—were rejected, because incorporating such subjectivity would compromise the goal of demystifying replication.[15] Color-based concerns of the outside world, of philology and art, might spark efforts to represent the whole concept of color, but attention to such matters would interfere with replicable measurement.

The ISCC Reviews Joseph Albers

Thus Albers and the authors of *Color: A Guide to Basic Facts and Concepts* shared an underlying concern: the articulation of rules to guide the use of color. But while *Interaction of Color* incorporated information established by scientific experiment, such as the work of the nineteenth-century manufacturing chemist Michel-Eugène Chevreul (1786–1889), the meteorologist Wilhelm Bezold (1873–1907), and the psychophysicists Ernst Heinrich Weber (1795–1878) and Gustav Theodor Fechner (1801–1887), Albers's search began with more personal consciousness and sensory experience. The ISCC scientists, for their part, were concerned with numbers rather than form; their search was for a means to guarantee the stability of any color experience rather than to highlight individuality.

As Brenda Danilowitz has noted, the idiosyncratic format of *Interaction of Color* made it a difficult book to review. Whether approaching the volume as a work of art or as a work about teaching art, reviewers were reluctant to analyze its content, at least in the earliest editions. One exception was a review by the artist Donald Judd in *Arts Magazine*, which emphasized Albers's indebtedness to Chevreul and wondered whether both the techniques and technical knowledge Albers offered might someday become outdated or outmoded, as certain of Chevreul's ideas had.[16] Would new methods for teaching color emerge as teachers absorbed Albers's ideas and combined them with others, or as art objects changed?

Another exception, very different in tone and approach, was the 1964 review of *Interaction of Color* that appeared in the *ISCC Newsletter*. Information in the archives of the Josef and Anni Albers Foundation, especially meeting programs and offprints, suggests that Albers knew of the ISCC, although we know nothing specific about his attention to its work. This review, however, provides concrete evidence of the ISCC's interest in Albers's work. The main portion of the review was written by Randall M. Hanes, a coauthor of *Color: A Guide to Basic Facts and Concepts*. As much as the review itself, the choice of reviewer is key in this discussion of the art–science divide at the time in terms of approaches to color.

Randall M. Hanes (1920–1994) was a graduate of Franklin and Marshall College and received a Ph.D. in psychology from Johns Hopkins University in 1950, writing a dissertation on physiological optics. He served as the chairman of ISCC's "Subcommittee for Problem 20" and as a director on ISCC's board, as well as a voting delegate on the board from the American Psychological Association. According to the biographical information in *Color: A Guide to Basic Facts and Concepts*, in 1964, when his review of *Interaction of Color* was published, he was employed at the Applied Physics Laboratory at Johns Hopkins.[17]

Hanes begins his review by remarking, as other reviewers had, on the "unusual format," of the book, calling attention to its great size, weight, cost, and the comparatively small quantity of text. He notes the high production value of the images, a practical detail that would be of interest to ISCC members, and quotes Albers's claim that *Interaction of Color* is "a record of an experimental way of studying color and of teaching color, placing 'practice before theory.'"[18] Hanes does not comment on this assertion, although it is clear from the review that he regarded the eighty-one colored plates in Albers's book as separate from the text and commentary rather than the integral experimental data Albers understood them to be. He praises several images as "mostly excellent," particularly for their contrast effects, and calls several studies "well executed."[19] However, his comments suggest that this assessment refers to the aesthetic quality of the images rather than their ability to demonstrate the principles Albers claimed for them. This impression is supported by his clear preference for the more figurative images such as the "Leaf Studies" and the prints of torn paper assembled to replicate Old Master paintings. Other illustrations, he says, "were ineffective for me," further suggesting that his judgments relate to the aesthetic quality rather than didactic capabilities of the images.[20] There is no indication in the review that Hanes was aware of Albers's reputation as a teacher of art; perhaps he considered this an irrelevant detail for the ISCC readership.

Hanes may not have considered art aesthetics his métier, but the application of laws from physics to describe color was. He is more critical of Albers's statements about color than of his assertions regarding the visual appeal of the artwork. In general, Hanes says, the text descriptions are confused, illogical, and full of errors of fact. He singles out Albers's statements about the contextual nature of color perception as a general illustration of this complaint, and expresses special concern for his explanation of certain scientific or optical effects. The mistakes Hanes cites range from a statement about the constancy of "Coca-Cola red" over time and in different geographical areas, to an assertion that all reflected colors—not only white—contain all other colors. For someone with a background in laboratory studies of the physics and chemistry of color, such statements were unequivocally false.

Hanes also offers detailed objections to several of Albers's assertions about the physical laws of color or color phenomena. For example, he cites Albers's demonstration of the Bezold effect—an optical illusion in which one color appears as two different ones owing to the adjacent color—as a presentation that was "ineffective for me."[21] In one illustration of the Bezold effect, Albers offers a pair of horizontally striped columns, one using red, pink, gray, and black, the other using red, pink, gray and white (fig. 10). He notes that in the image with white on the right, the red-pink-gray portions look lighter in color and weight than they do on the left, where they are surrounded by black.[22]

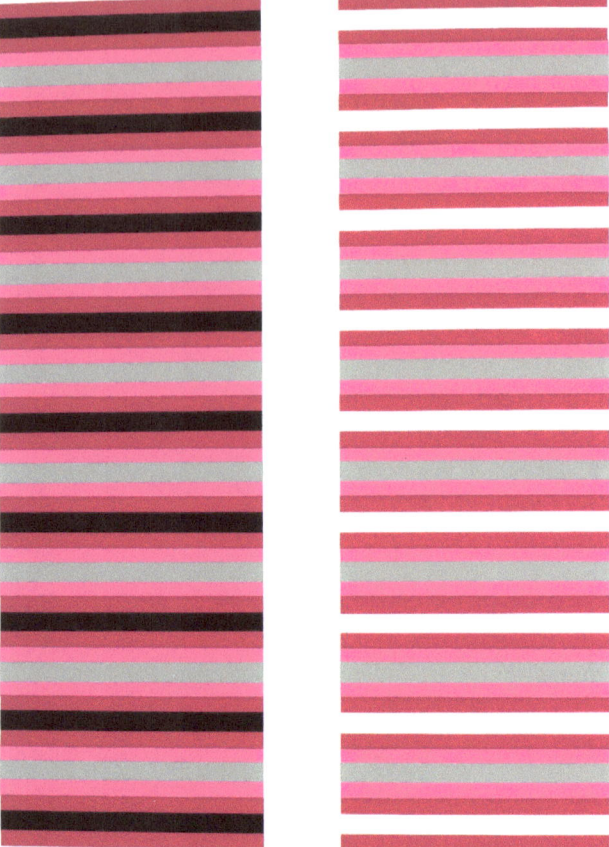

Figure 10: "Optical Mixture—The Bezold Effect." Josef Albers, *Interaction of Color* (New Haven: Yale University Press, 1963), Plate XIII-2. Image courtesy the Josef and Anni Albers Foundation/Yale University Press.

In the review, Hanes also objects to Albers's statement about the relativity of color, claiming that "this approach can lead only to a poor understanding of the phenomenon" that scientists call color adjacency (visual variability owing to placement).[23] Hanes complained about Albers's general reliance on analogy (it looks *like* this, rather than it *is* this) to support his statements, calling this a form of argument that does little to advance general knowledge about the phenomena of color.[24]

Hanes's position reflected significant differences between science and art in both expectations and approach. Analogy was in fact a basis of Albers's teaching method; for him, such connections between personal experience and the larger world were a useful pedagogical approach.[25] Yet for exactly this reason—reliance on the unquantifiably personal—explanation by analogy has no place in the modern, nonspeculative physical sciences. To Hanes—and probably to many readers of the *ISCC Newsletter*—teaching such misconceptions as those found in *Interaction of Color* would not lead to discovery, flexible imagination, or invention. While the publication, Hanes acknowledges, might represent a monument to the career of the author, its instructional value for those students interested in color was less certain. Perhaps more important, Hanes did not judge it to be a scientifically dynamic work.

Before the review was published, either Hanes himself, or perhaps the editors of the *ISCC Newsletter*, requested further comments from Deane B. Judd (1900–1972; no relation to Donald Judd), an acclaimed and versatile color expert. Judd's comments were published in the same issue. Throughout his professional life Judd, a physicist by training, wrote extensively about color vision and the industrial applications of color science. In 1963 he was chairperson of the ISCC Problems Committee as well as chairperson of its subcommittee on color nomenclature. He was also known to have a broad familiarity with historical explanations of color perception and nonempirical explanation of color phenomena.

Like Hanes, Judd highlights confusions and errors in Albers's book, including what Hanes had called "a fundamental difference between a technical and a non-technical approach."[26] He focuses particularly on Albers's section about the Weber–Fechner Law, which explains that the strength of a visual sensation (i.e., perception) varies logarithmically as the strength of the stimulus increases in intensity—a number-based description of a visual phenomenon well known to artists. For the purpose of his inquiry, Albers, in *Interaction of Color*, interprets the underlying question as: "What is necessary to produce a visually even progression in mixture?"[27] To derive the answer, Albers instructs the student to build up two rectangles from layers of a single color ink or transparent colored paper, gradually decreasing the portion overlaid with new color. One sample should rely on an arithmetic (1-2-3-4) increase in the number of layers applied, the other on a geometric (1-2-4-8) increase (fig. 11). In the first, arithmetic example (on the left), Albers explains, the layers of color added will appear to have decreased, as there is little visual difference between the two deeper shades at the bottom of that column. In the right-hand, geometrically calculated image, the colors appear to maintain an even separation throughout.

Without specifically remarking on the analogic basis of Albers's presentation, Judd makes clear that he finds both the explanation and examples problemat-

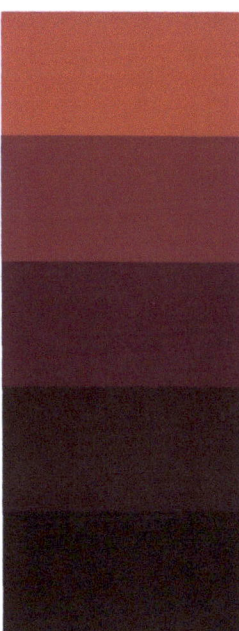

Figure 11: "The Weber-Fechner Law." Josef Albers, *Interaction of Color*, Plate XX-1. Image courtesy the Josef and Anni Albers Foundation/Yale University Press.

ic. Albers's experimental study is not related to the Weber–Fechner law, Judd emphasizes, because he describes a progression taking place in light absorption when, in fact, the law refers to progression in luminance (brightness). While Albers correctly notes that the color scale in the image on the left is perceived as having smaller gradations between the colors of the darker end and those of the lighter end, Judd insists that this is not an example of the law he references. The Weber–Fechner law offers no guidance about the behavior of ordinary grounds such as dyes or pigments; the law concerns light alone, and Judd adds that Albers "is as ignorant" of the studies of gray scales made since Fechner's time "as he is of the meaning of the Weber–Fechner law that he cites."[28] Judd also points to other statements made by Albers which, if not exactly wrong as descriptions of visual impressions, lack the technical basis to qualify as valuable, scientifically based description.

Discussion

Clearly, Albers was not a color scientist. What, then, is the value of his studies? What was he teaching, with his emphasis on subjectivity and analogy? An answer to these questions was suggested by an anonymous reviewer of *Interaction of Color*, writing for the journal *Vision Research*, who concluded that

> …though the text of Josef Albers is clearly geared to the artist and is in fact virtually incomprehensible to the scientist, nevertheless the demonstrations of interaction effects in color contained in his quite extraordinary study constitute the most effective ones available anywhere today…. Quantitative physiological approaches have a long task ahead before they will be able to come to grips with the subjective color universe displayed before us in our everyday world, and captured so splendidly by Albers and [Johannes] Itten [Albers's colleague at the Bauhaus].[29]

In other words, Albers may have been thinking and acting on a level that the color sciences, as practiced in 1963, could not accommodate, just as he could not accommodate the work or perspective of color scientists. As Hanes's critique of Albers's book suggests, *Interaction of Color* and *Color: A Guide to Basic Facts and Concepts* highlight differences in expectations concerning knowledge about color that were typical of the art–science dichotomy as it existed in the mid-twentieth century.

Although we know nothing of Hanes's engagement with art theories or art practices, we do know that Albers's research into color included his study of chemical and physical theories of color, and that his efforts to understand the congruencies between art and science included reading as well as experimentation. The archive at the Josef and Anni Albers Foundation includes materials he consulted in his studies, ranging from offprints from academic or professional journals, to articles and essays written for a knowledgeable but nontechnical public, to popular writing. Albers's own professional life—including twenty-five years of writing and presenting lectures about color perception—allowed him to absorb and personalize the information of his research.

If all explanations of color could be placed on a spectrum, with fully quantifiable descriptions at one end and sensation-based ones at the other, *Color: A Guide to Basic Facts and Concepts* would rest near the quantified end and *Interaction of Color* would be closer to the sensation side. Neither book, however—and by extension, the scientists of the ISCC on one side and Albers and his students on the other—would be perched at the absolute edge, nor at the center. But if, in 1963, color scientists engaged number-based identification systems to ensure that color sensation could be quantified and systematized, Albers, like many artists, gave more idiosyncratic meanings to color sensation and systematization.

The driving force of the ISCC was the need to share information not only from lab to lab, but from discipline to discipline. As with any standardization effort, it was important to be able to codify all components and to remove uncontrollable variables. The best means to accomplish this was a philosophical or mathematical reduction of all information to the least number of facts required, and the establishment of relationships among those facts. This method yielded a common or consistent vocabulary for students and practitioners involved in creating products in the factory and preparing them for the sales floor.

Albers's charge to his students, by contrast, was to create meaningful works of art that did not control all aspects of the viewer's reaction, to manage color without standardizing its form. He did not consider the mathematical quantification of color information—the goal of the ISCC—an unqualified benefit. Within mid-twentieth century discussions of color and the art–science relationship, scientists often pointed to Goethe's insistence on the irrelevance of Newtonian mathematics to a useful or worldly understanding of color as a marker of antiscientific approaches. In *Interaction of Color* (and other publications) Albers offers only indirect criticism of scientific descriptions of color—quite unlike, for example, the emphatic rejection of artistic subjectivity displayed by the authors of the *Guide*. In rejecting scientific ideas of standardization Albers (like his former Bauhaus colleagues) was focusing less on science than on academic traditions in art that emphasized the rules of perspective and the "facts" learned in life drawing as the foundation of an artist's training. The ISCC's goals of standardization and codification were not so dissimilar from the goals of the European academies of art, such as the Paris Academy of Painting and Sculpture (Académie Royale de Peinture et de Sculpture) or the Royal Academy of Arts in London. Established in parallel with the academies of sciences, the academic art programs emphasized fact-based education as a prelude to later artistic production. For Albers, by contrast, the real work of the artist did not begin when experimentation ended. As *Interaction of Color* demonstrates, for Albers the experiments never end.

Just as members of the ISCC subcommittee discussed the need to separate fact from fancy, Albers called for a separation of what he called "factual facts" from "actual facts."[30] While a "factual fact" may be taught in the classroom (or valorized by color scientists working to quantify the visual experience), an "actual fact" is directly connected to experience. Albers's interest was the "actual facts," what viewer experience shows to be true, rather than what the scientist or mathematician declares to be so. In lectures and other publications, he explained the difference somewhat mischievously. An example is provided in his pedagogical exercise "1 + 1 = 3" (fig. 12).[31]

Take two colored rectangular shapes, he suggests. Considered separately, the shapes demonstrate the idea that 1 + 1 = 2. This is a "factual fact." However, if you arrange the two shapes parallel to each other, and consider the image from the left edge of the left rectangle to the right edge of the right rectangle, the space between the two colored blocks, which permits recognition of the two blocks, also represents a block. Together, the visual sequence demonstrates that 1 + 1 = 3, an "actual fact."[32] Albers's example of the Bezold effect (fig. 10, above) shows, similarly, how the white stripe combines visually with the white paper to create an "actual fact" of eight pairs of red-pink-gray-pink-red, rather than a single striped column. To Albers, success in artistic practice was based on just such a blending of materials with immediate experiences, not on the inert "factual facts" of the scientist.

Why Study Color?

Albers, like other mid-twentieth-century art teachers, saw a challenge in the need to convince students to abandon preconceived notions about color, color combinations, and the relationships between colors, particularly (but not exclusively) on a planar surface. For Albers, the success of *Interaction of Color* as a teaching tool was due to its demand that the reader or user ignore current and broadly held assumptions about the primacy of the sciences and the ways those assumptions influenced arts and culture.

But just as these two 1963 publications, along with the response to one of them, show differences in the understandings and outcomes of science and art, they demonstrate the ways in which the ultimate goals of science and art are

Figure 12: Josef Albers's demonstration that 1+1 can equal 3 (or more). The top image shows that 1+1 = 2. In the image below it, the addition of a space between the two bars (all of which remain, nevertheless, as a single unit) shows that 1+1 can also equal 3. The bottom two examples show that two bars can be positioned to create four "arms" of either equal or unequal sizes. From Josef Albers, "One Plus One Equals Three and More: Factual Facts and Actual Facts," in *Search versus Re-Search* (Hartford, CT: Trinity College Press, 1969), 18. Image courtesy the Watkinson Library, Trinity College, Hartford, CT.

similar. The art-color community (if such a thing existed in 1963) was concerned with issues of basic information, just as the color-science community was. Each chose and defined relevant facts and the information all practitioners must know, according to their own concerns. Determining the mathematical definition of luminance permitted physicists and chemists, color engineers and laboratory managers to speak to one another about this component of color without confusion. For an artist or a viewer of artwork, the significance of this mathematical description might be negligible. For Albers, the more critical concerns were understanding the relative appearance of colors (such as the ways in which the interaction between adjacent colors affects the visual perception of each) and understanding the rules of this contextuality. For the artist, personal expression and creativity do not require a knowledge of color formulas or mathematical calibrations of hue-value-chroma. Artistic creativity and experimentation, as taught by *Interaction of Color*, require an understanding of materials and the way they work together. With this information, each project can begin with a blank page and the question, "What if?"

Today, even popular writing about the problematic relationship of color in science and art often characterizes its essence as an argument between calculations, arranged in *this* way, and sentiments, organized in *that* way. We give personality to these differences in approach and attitude when we label the assumed conflict of artists versus scientists as "Goethe versus Newton." In that fabled disagreement, Goethe's color theories stand for anti-Newtonian stances that predated Goethe's—and occasionally even Newton's—time. We are told that the conflict may be resolved in our minds by recognizing that Goethe's mathematical abilities were not sophisticated enough to allow for a true understanding of Newton's *Opticks* and that Newton's belief in a mathematical explanation for all phenomena led him to misinterpret differences between the celestial colors of light, and the terrestrial colors of earthly bodies. This notion of incompatibility between the two natural philosophers has become a touchstone for discussions of the dichotomy between science and art. Discussions of Goethe's theories in particular often focus on the vehemence with which he rejected Newtonian mathematical explanations, or else they dismiss his views as excessively combative and therefore incompatible with modern scientific practices.[33]

Yet while aspects of the art–science divide undoubtedly persist, its mid-twentieth-century invocation, as evidenced by the Albers–ISCC debate (or at least the implicit debate initiated by the ISCC) was a more nuanced matter than we often believe. Overly simple accounts effectively dismiss subtleties by highlighting the quantitative nature of the ISCC approach in general, and the way the *Guide* addressed the "problem," in contrast to the qualitative approach of *Inter-*

action of Color. Yet any assessments that assume an underlying incompatibility between science and art and therefore the pointlessness of further consideration are incomplete. For the questions both books set out to answer are not, in fact, so distant: What information do you need to do your work, whatever that work may be? How should you organize that information? What do you want it to tell you?

Acknowledgments

I am very grateful for the assistance of many people as I prepared this essay, including Brenda Danilowitz, chief curator, and Jeannette Redensek, catalogue raisonné researcher, at the Josef and Anni Albers Foundation; Jo Ann Taylor, longstanding ISCC member and former board member; Marsha Mills, archival specialist at the Hagley Museum and Library; Richard Ring, curator at the Watkinson Library, Trinity College; Vanja Malloy; and several anonymous reviewers.

Notes

1. The editions I use are Isaac Newton, *Opticks; Or, A Treatise of the Reflections, Refractions, Inflections & Colours of Light. Based on the 4th Ed.*, London, 1730 (New York: Dover Publications, 1952) and Johann Wolfgang von Goethe, *Farbenlehre*, edited by Gerhard Ott, 6th ed., 5 vols. (Stuttgart: Freies Geistesleben, 1997); there are many others of both works. On the debate between Goethe and Newton see, e.g., the chapter introductions in David L. MacAdam, *Sources of Color Science* (Cambridge, MA: MIT Press, 1970).
2. Josef Albers, *Interaction of Color* (New Haven: Yale University Press, 1963).
3. Robert W. Burnham, Randall M. Hanes, and C. James Bartleson, *Color: A Guide to Basic Facts and Concepts* (New York: Wiley, 1963); "ISCC Aims and Purposes," accessed November 12, 2013, http://iscc.org/organization/aims.php.
4. R. M. Hanes, "The Interaction of Color by Josef Albers: A Review with an Addendum by D. B. Judd," *ISCC Newsletter* 172 (August 1964): 20–26.
5. Brenda Danilowitz, "A Short History of Josef Albers's *Interaction of Color*," in *Intersecting Colors: Josef Albers and His Contemporaries*, ed. Vanja Malloy (Amherst, MA: Amherst College Press, 2015); Frederick A Horowitz and Brenda Danilowitz, *Josef Albers: To Open Eyes: The Bauhaus, Black Mountain College, and Yale* (London: Phaidon, 2006).
6. Regina Lee Blaszczyk, *The Color Revolution* (Cambridge, MA.: MIT Press, 2012).
7. Albers, *Interaction of Color*, 1.
8. Albers, *Interaction of Color*, 5.
9. See "ISCC Aims and Purposes" in Dorothy Nickerson, "Fifty Years of the Inter-Society Color Council. I. Formation and Early Years," *Color Research and Application* 7:1 (Spring 1982): 5–11.

10. Royal B. Farnham, "Results of a Questionnaire on Color in Art Education," *Journal of the Optical Society of America* 32 (December 1942): 720–26.

11. Nickerson, "Fifty Years of the Inter-Society Color Council," 7.

12. Burnham, Hanes, and Bartleson, *Color: A Guide to Basic Facts and Concepts*, v.

13. Burnham, Hanes, and Bartleson, *Color: A Guide to Basic Facts and Concepts*, 1.

14. Burnham, Hanes, and Bartleson, *Color: A Guide to Basic Facts and Concept*, 5.

15. Burnham, Hanes, and Bartleson, *Color: A Guide to Basic Facts and Concepts*, viii.

16. Donald Judd, "Albers and Chevreul," *Arts Magazine* 38:2 (November 1963): 66–67, 73, 75. See also M. E. Chevreul, *De la loi du contraste simultané des couleurs, et de l'assortiment des objets colorés, considéré d'après cette loi* (Paris: Pitois-Levrault et Cie, 1839).

17. "Dr. Randall M. Hanes (1920-94)," *Public Opinion* (Chambersburg, PA), August 31, 1994, sec. Obituary; quoted at http://bit.ly/1FZR3sY. For other biographical information, see *ISCC Newsletter* 168 (November-December 1963), 13; available at http://www.iscc.org/Newsletters/ISCCNews168.pdf, accessed 27 July 2015.

18. R. M. Hanes, "Interaction of Color by Josef Albers: A Review," *ISCC Newsletter* 172 (July–August 1964), 20; http://www.iscc.org/Newsletters/ISCCNews172.pdf, accessed July 27, 2015.

19. Hanes, "Interaction of Color by Josef Albers," 21.

20. Hanes, "Interaction of Color by Josef Albers," 21.

21. Hanes, "Interaction of Color by Josef Albers," 21.

22. Albers, *Interaction of Color*, figure XIII-2.

23. Hanes, "Interaction of Color by Josef Albers," 21.

24. For example, "Just as the knowledge of acoustics does not make one musical—neither on the productive nor on the appreciative side—so no color system by itself can develop one's sensitivity for color." Hanes, "The Interaction of Color by Josef Albers," 21.

25. Horowitz and Danilowitz, *Josef Albers: To Open Eyes: The Bauhaus, Black Mountain College, and Yale*, esp. 73–97.

26. Hanes, "The Interaction of Color by Josef Albers," 26.

27. Albers, *Interaction of Color*, 55.

28. Hanes, "The Interaction of Color by Josef Albers," 25.

29. "Some Recent Books on Colour," *Vision Research* 6 (1966): 120.

30. Josef Albers, "One Plus One Equals Three and More: Factual Facts and Actual Facts," in *Search versus Re-Search* (Hartford, CT: Trinity College Press, 1969), 17–23.

31. Albers, "One Plus One Equals Three," see also "Albers as a Teacher" video accompanying *Interaction of Color* app.

32. Albers, "One Plus One Equals Three," and *Interaction of Color*, 71–72.

33. See especially volumes 4 and 5 of Johann Wolfgang von Goethe, *Zur Farbenlehre: Historischer Teil*, ed. Gertrud and Gerhard Ott, 6th ed. (Stuttgart: Freies Geistesleben, 1997).

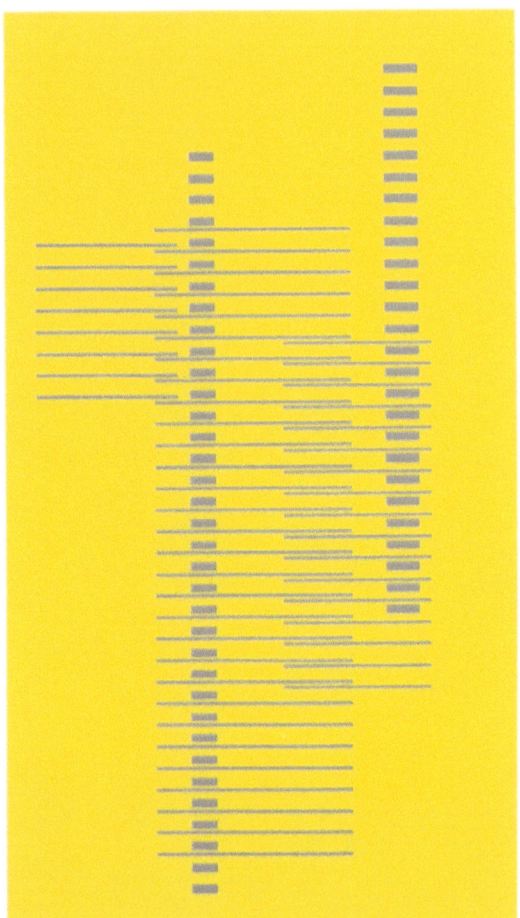 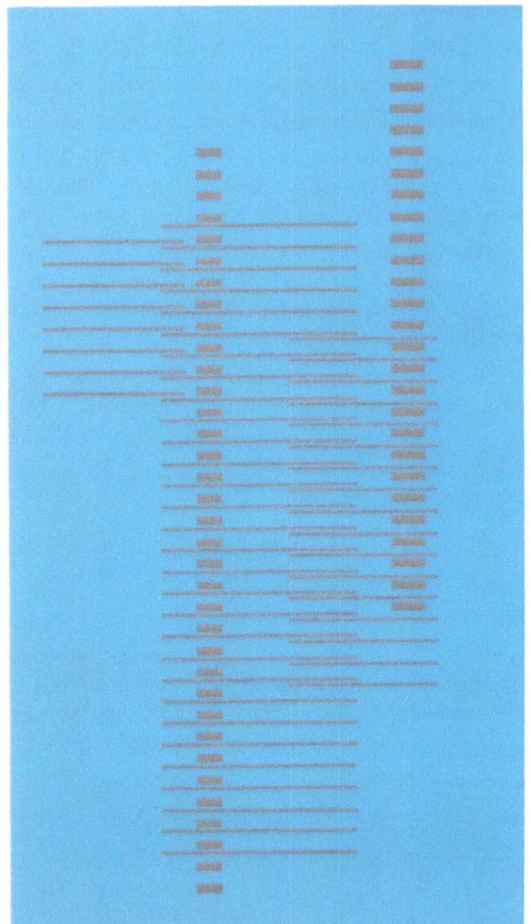

Cat. 14: Josef Albers, *Formulation : Articulation*, Folio I / Folder 6, 1972. Screenprint, 15 x 20 in. (38.1 x 50.8 cm). Mead Art Museum, Amherst College, gift of the Alan M. Sternlieb Study Collection (1979.103.1.6.a).

More Than Parallel Lines:
Thoughts on Gestalt, Albers, and the Bauhaus

Karen Koehler

An undated sketch in the collection of the Anni and Josef Albers Foundation bears a striking resemblance to the well-known Gestalt diagram about the nature of human perception (figs. 13 and 14). First published by Edgar Rubin in 1914, the Gestalt illustration asks the basic question: Do you see a vase or two faces? The point is that there is no absolute answer—what we see depends on what our brains decide is true at a given moment. This simple exercise has been used to demonstrate that we need to interrogate the concrete actualities of images and objects. There are, in fact, different realities—one based on materiality and one based in perception. The drawing by Albers, although perhaps more complex because of the irregularity of the curving lines, suggests that he, too, was working out ideas about how humans perceive figure-ground relationships.

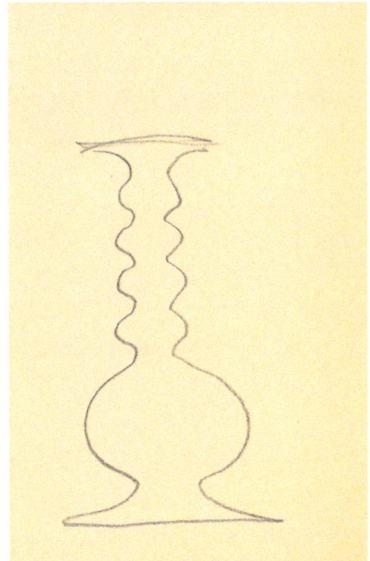
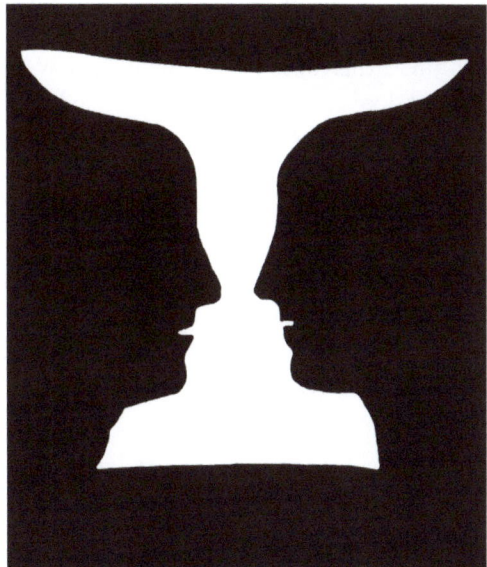

Figure 13 (left): Josef Albers, Untitled sketch, n.d. Drawing on paper. The Josef and Anni Albers Foundation (1976.3.547).

Figure 14 (right): Figure and Ground Study, after Edgar Rubin, *Synsoplevede Figurer: Studier i psykologisk Analyse* (Copenhagen: Gyldendal, 1915).

Taken broadly, these images raise what is perhaps the most essential philosophical question: What is real? And, by extension: Where is meaning located—in materiality, or in our brains? This complex exchange between our cognitive perceptions and the physical substance of objects or images was at the core of the phenomenological problems that interested not only the Gestalt psychologists, but also many Bauhaus teachers as they sought to radicalize the teaching and making of art. As Albers wrote in an essay for Bauhaus 2/3, in 1928, two separate elements are able to form "at least one interesting relation that is more than just the sum of those elements."[1] Similar to the oft-cited phrase that the "whole is more than the sum of its parts," the Bauhaus teacher aligned his analysis of formal relationships with the language of Gestalt psychology concurrently evolving in Germany.

Or did he?

Connections between Gestalt psychology and the pedagogies and artistic practices of the famous art school, the Bauhaus, have been debated for years—most recently in a series of published emails between a group of Bauhaus scholars and the descendants of the original Gestalt psychologists that were published in the journal *Gestalt Theory*.[2] We do know that there were at least a couple of definite interfaces. In the 1930–31 school year, Karlfried Graf von Dürkheim came from Leipzig to hold a series of lectures on Gestalt at the Bauhaus. Detlef Mertins suggested that it was Hannes Meyer, director of the Bauhaus from 1928 to 1930, who wanted to expose students to connections between "the psychic and the social," although the invitation to Dürkheim may have come from the student council.[3] According to Hannes Beckmann, who was then a student: "Up until this time design problems were more or less solved on the feeling level. It looked as if the artist asked the scientists for reassurance that they were on the right track. The Gestalt psychologists had, after all, for years investigated how we perceive and interpret form and color in the mind."[4] Another possible connection, although one based on anecdotal recollection, is a lecture in 1929 at the Bauhaus reportedly given by Karl Duncker, the assistant to the one of the leading figures of the Berlin School of Gestalt psychology, Wolfgang Köhler. Duncker had extended the study of induced motion, central to Gestalt theory, into questions of memory function and environmental perception, and Marianne Teuber wrote in 1973 of the influence of this lecture on the work of Paul Klee.[5]

Others have written about similar points of contact, influences, common concepts, and parallel interests. For example, there has been some focus on connections between Gestalt theory and the pedagogies of both Klee and Wassily Kandinsky who contributed to the *Vorkurs*, the foundations courses at the Bauhaus—the cornerstone of the reformation of art education at the school. In the *Vorkurs*, instead of mimetic copying, students were taught to focus on the abstract properties of color, form, and material.[6] Yet, outside of a few suggestions of formal comparisons, or second hand stories of the artists mentioning Gestalt, documents that give evidence of precise exchanges between the Bauhaus and the psychologists remain elusive. Inaccurate narratives about the anti-historical nature of the Bauhaus have confused the situation, and the reliance on memoirs or recollections have led to a weak analysis of what any connections between the institutions might have meant.

In the 1919 *Bauhaus Manifesto*, Walter Gropius (the founder and first director of the Bauhaus) spoke of the *vielgliedrige Gestalt*, or "composite character," of the work of architecture. In the *Manifesto*—a proclamation attached to the first official Bauhaus program of study—Gropius wrote of the need for architects, painters and sculptors to come together in the revolutionary aftermath of World War I to create the total work of art.[7] Gropius's idealized concept of the work of architecture as a *Gesamtkunstwerk* could be seen as generally Gestalt-like in its holistic vision. In a collection of Bauhaus reminiscences from 1970, T. Lux Feininger wrote of the connections between the Bauhaus and ideas of *Gestaltung*, or totalities, in Gropius's early thinking, and in the designation of the Bauhaus as a *Hochschule für Gestaltung*.[8] In a largely ignored passage of the founding program, Gropius also wrote of his intention to bring to the Bauhaus "training in science and theory." This included not only the science of materials and of color, but also "art history—not presented in the sense of a history of styles, but rather to further active understanding of historical working methods and techniques."[9] Gropius linked scientific and art historical theory in the very first publication outlining the directions of his radical new art school, suggesting that he was aware of current debates in the discipline of art history, between *Kunstgeschichte* (art history) and *Kunstwissenschaft* (the scientific study of art).[10]

In an interview recorded in 1968, nearly five decades later, Albers mentioned an exchange he had in Dessau, with the Gestalt psychologists about his ideas on form. According to Albers, the scientists only confirmed his conclusions that in early childhood we have clearer recognition of three dimensions over two dimensions.[11] Hearing Albers speak these words makes them seem more factual, but there is still a problem here. Does it matter that we are reconstructing this history based on reminiscences? Are we missing the relational aesthetic—what might be seen as a requisite for any Gestaltish-art history of the Bauhaus?

I'd like to take a somewhat different approach, and accept for a moment that we are looking at parallel institutions; think of the Bauhaus as one straight line and the Berlin School of Gestalt psychology as another. What would it take to see them as separate but relational, as two parts of a linked historical cluster? What are the connections between these tandem histories and the work of Josef Albers—that is, how might we in fact *find* the Gestalt in some of his art?

◘

The Berlin School began in the first decade of the twentieth century and was firmly established in the immediate postwar period with the appointment of Wolfgang Köhler and Max Wertheimer to posts at the University of Berlin.[12] The Bauhaus was established in 1919 with the appointment of Gropius, although the school was in many ways an outgrowth of prewar developments in the teaching of the applied arts, as well as institutions like the Deutscher Werkbund.[13] In Germany at the time, the relatively new field of psychology—which combined elements of the human and natural sciences—was housed in departments of philosophy. The need to establish experimental laboratories was a continual challenge. The conservatism of the German university system also made it difficult to operate as a laboratory science within the humanistic discipline of philosophy and to introduce the new concepts of Gestalt, which studied human and natural phenomena with the goal of integrating the inanimate object with what was perceived in the mind into a single scientific structure. The Bauhaus was an institution that merged the study of aesthetics with the making of objects, combining theories of form with requisite work in one of the craft studios. Gropius also challenged conservative academic structures when he combined the Weimar School of Arts and Crafts with the Academy of Fine Arts. Each studio at the Bauhaus was led by a craft master and a form master, in order to bring together instruction in the applied arts and the aesthetics of form. Thus, both the Berlin School and the Bauhaus were committed to "role hybridization"; the psychologists were to be philosophers and experimental practitioners, while the Bauhäusler were studying to be both artists and craftsmen (and women) or designers.[14]

Both the Gestalt psychologists and the Bauhaus artists lost their positions when the National Socialists came to power; many were forced into exile in the United States and elsewhere. Some of the scientists and artists remained in Germany, and despite the reputation of the Bauhaus and the Berlin School as standing in opposition to fascism, continued to work under the Third Reich. Tools of Weimar psychology were used by the Nazis to determine the suitability of individuals to join the SS, and the plans of Auschwitz were drawn by a Bauhaus-trained architect.[15] After World War II, and during much of the Cold War, both Gestalt psychology and the Bauhaus were historically over-simplified, frequently misunderstood, and eventually fell out of favor—replaced by behaviorism and post-modernism, respectively. Over two decades of new scholarship has transformed the scholarly position of the Bauhaus, including two comprehensive exhibitions in 2009. Rigorous and meticulous books, articles and essay collections began to emerge after German reunification, and these complex analyses of individual artists, mediums, and practices have exposed a different and more diverse Bauhaus, with a complicated historical path.[16] Yet, the "Bauhaus" is still used as a stylistic term, which can somehow stand in for modernism around the globe. The term "Gestalt" was appropriated by what came to be called "Gestalt therapy," a psychotherapeutic practice that emerged in the 1940s, became especially popular for its "holistic approach" during the 1960s and 70s, and continues as a clinical practice today. Although there is some shared lineage, Gestalt therapy bears almost no resemblance to the rigorous experimental science of the Berlin School.[17]

But the question remains: Are these sample elements of their parallel histories simply the result of the same historical and political trajectories? Are they really commonalities or are they rather coincidences? In other words, do the similarities have any meaning?

The principal scientists to come out of the Berlin Gestalt group—Max Wertheimer and Wolfgang Köhler, as well as Kurt Koffka—rejected previous psychological theories about the role of sensations in the mitigation of materiality and perception. Sensations, according to the Gestalt school, are physical things; they exist in actuality. Perceptions, by contrast, are classified as mental events, and while we may regard them as faithful representations of objective reality, they are not. Frederic Schwartz explains this idea succinctly: "Gestalt psychology represents a theory about the way sensations are ordered by the mind, how sensations (which are external) are turned into perceptions (which define the juncture of living being and world, subject and object.)"[18] Or as Mitchell Ash insists, Wertheimer, Köhler and Koffka never actually claimed "the whole is *more* than the sum of its parts." For the Gestaltists, when we experience objects—and relationships between objects—these are *"fundamentally different* from collections of sensations, parts, or pieces."[19] What we perceive is based upon structures, upon expected or found patterns of relationships. They were studying the aesthetics of what we recognize as an inherent order to things. Gestalt is not so much about the whole, as it is about relationality—about seeing patterns and forming connections.

We know that Josef Albers was intensely interested in the ways in which we perceive colors, separate from their physical realities—in this way, he was concerned with the Gestalt of colors. As other essays in this volume show, the

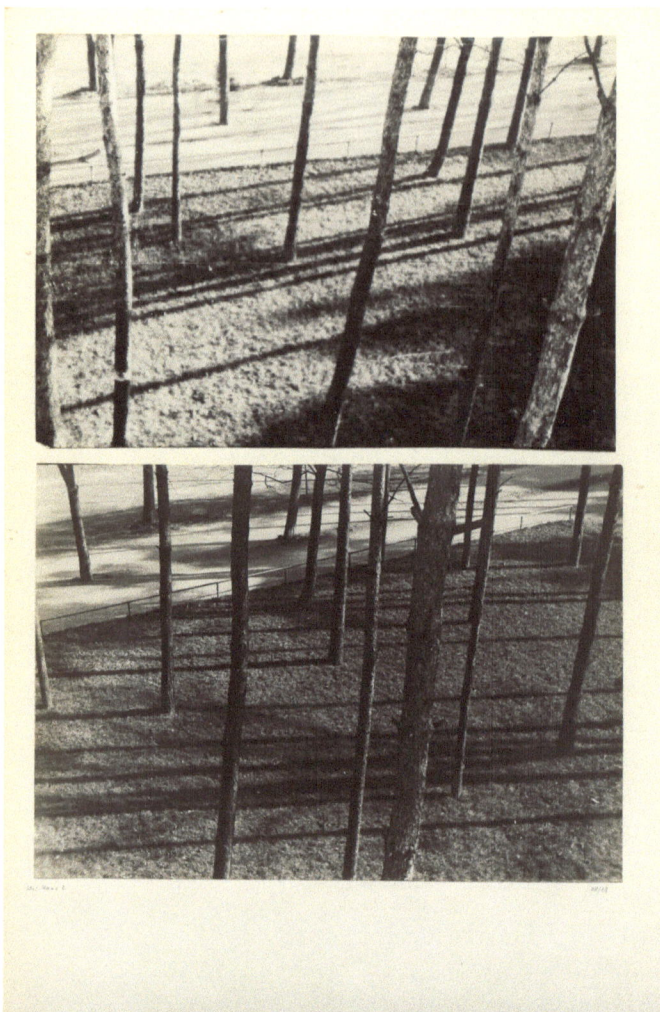

Figure 15: Josef Albers, *Bei Haus 2 (At Home 2)*, 1928-1929. Two gelatin silver prints mounted on paperboard. Solomon R. Guggenheim Museum, New York, gift of the Josef and Anni Albers Foundation (96.4502.4).

origins of his approach to color was complex, multi-causal, and principally the result of his experimentations in his post-Bauhaus years.[20] Instead, this essay will turn to examples of Albers's Bauhaus designs in order to demonstrate his interest in what the Gestalt psychologists identified as our inherent cognitive tendency to *constellate*—that is, we perceive separate shapes in terms of patterns rather than individually. We conceptually group together forms due to their proximation, and we see elements that look alike as belonging together. I believe that the best evidence of Gestalt at the Bauhaus is in the way that Albers anticipated and manipulated this perceptual phenomenon.

For example, in a work called *Bei Haus 2 (At Home 2)* from 1928-1929, Albers mounted two photographs, stacked, of trees and their shadows (fig. 15). There are two sets of patterns working simultaneously—the bare trees create a constellated pattern of vertical lines, while the shadows create a second set of horizontal lines that operate as a separate pattern. Which shadow comes from which tree is indistinguishable—and irrelevant. Furthermore, when seen together, the trees (or shadows) in each of the two photographs combine to create a shared relational structure that jumps from one image to the next. Significantly, these are photographs, not paintings. These relationships occurred in nature (botanical and atmospheric) and were made by nature (the mechanical and chemical properties of photography and the synapses of the brain). Albers saw them, captured them with his camera, and produced two gelatin silver prints. At first we see the phenomenon as simply objective—something that occurred in the physical world. However, the *doubling* effect of the two photographs demonstrates that they are, in fact, not something that simply occurred in the material world, or something that is sensed as natural phenomena. As the patterns move from one picture to the next, and create a structure of pure lines and shapes, it is clear that this abstracting phenomenon is a matter of perception.

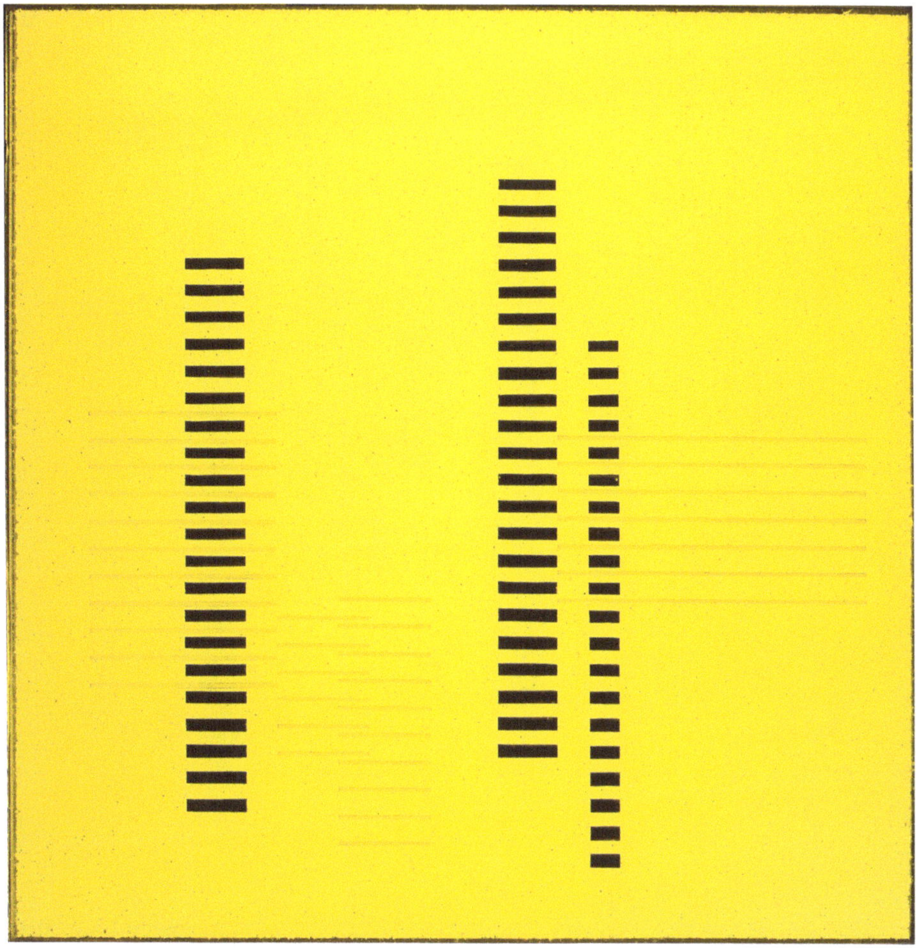

Figure 16: Josef Albers, *Hochbauten* [*Skyscrapers*], ca. 1929. Sandblasted glass with black paint, 13 3/8 x 13 1/8 in. (34 x 33.5 cm). The Josef and Anni Albers Foundation (1976.6.9).

This kind of patterning is precisely what Albers constructed in his "Skyscraper" series from 1929 (fig. 16). In these sandblasted glass paintings, Albers used a series of stacked horizontal shapes to create his forms. Yet, because of their repetition and their proximity, we read them first as a series of vertical shapes. It is only at the moment of the second, analytical look that we become aware that the "skyscraper" forms are made of identical horizontal forms.

This perceptual tendency to constellate shapes was demonstrated in illustrations for Wertheimer's article on "Gestalt laws" in an issue of *Psychologische Forschung* published as a Festschrift for Carl Stumpf in 1923. One example presents rows of circles and dots to reveal the organizing tendencies in vision, specifically the effects of proximity and similarity (fig. 17). Two other works by Albers from 1923—*Fruit Bowl*, or his *Tea Glass with Saucer and Stirrer*—show

Figure 17 (left): Excerpts from Max Wertheimer, "Untersuchungen zur Lehre von der Gestalt" ("Investigations on Gestalt Principles"), *Psychologische Forschung*, special issue (*Festschrift: Carl Stumpf*), 1923, 308–309. A translation of the text in this figure is given at note 21.

Figure 18 (top right): Josef Albers, *Fruit Bowl*, 1924. Silver-plated metal, glass, and wood, 3 5/8 x 16 3/4 in. (9.2 x 42.5 cm). Manufactured by Bauhaus Metal Workshop, Germany. Gift of Walter Gropius. The Museum of Modern Art (190.1958). Digital Image © The Museum of Modern Art/Licensed by SCALA/Art Resource, NY.

Figure 19 (bottom right): Josef Albers, *Tea glass with saucer and stirrer*, 1925. Heat resistant glass, chrome-plated steel, ebony, porcelain; glass: 2 1/4 x 3 1/2 in. (5.7 x 8.9 cm); saucer diameter: 4 1/4 in. (10.5 cm); stirrer: 4 x 1/2 in. (10.3 x 1.1 cm). The Josef and Anni Albers Foundation (2006.17.1).

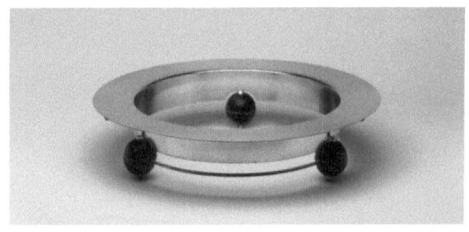

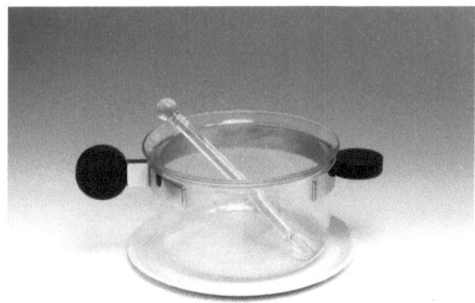

that he was also well aware of the relational, clustering properties of circles and spheres (figs. 18 and 19). We are drawn to see the black spheres in relationship to each other, despite their separation on either side of the glass forms, just as in the Wertheimer illustration where we concentrate on the circles of the same size, despite the sections between them, which are made of circles of a different size.[21]

Another example that expands the workings of these relational structures, and the foundational principals of perceptual organization, is one of Albers's best-known works, his *Stacking Tables* from 1927 (fig. 20). Both functional and playful, these tables not only have the same constellated characteristics of horizontal and vertical groupings, they are also dynamic—we can arrange (and perceive) the groupings according to proximities that we control. The "Gestalt switch" is thrown not only through pictorial experimentation, but also in a purposefully designed functional set of objects. Albers's tables make up a constantly shifting set of groupings, and because of the descending/ascending colored surfaces create a subtle perception of movement even when they are still. This perceptual phenomenon bares some resemblance to Max Wertheimer's groundbreaking 1912 experiments (fig. 21). Based on a complicated series of experiments with an apparatus known as the tachistoscope, Wertheimer proved that apparent (as

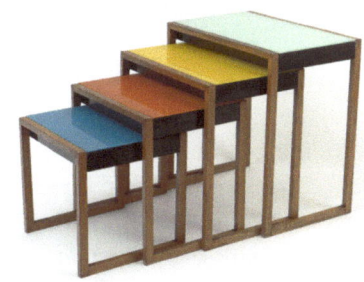

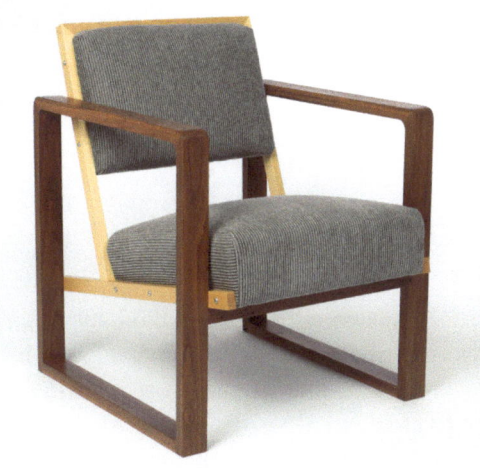

opposed to real) motion is a particular kind of visual illusion in which the subjects experience shapes in motion even though the stimuli are stationary.[22]

Some of the chairs designed by Albers, such as his armchair for Hans Ludwig and Margarete Oesler, Berlin, 1928, seem to play precisely with these ideas about perceived motion—enhanced in this case by the difference between the light and dark woods (fig. 22). According to Wertheimer, our brains perceive motion where there is none, and surely there is also a connection to this kind of perceived motion in the imagined weightlessness of many Bauhaus chair designs—not only those designed by Albers, but also by Marcel Breuer and Ludwig Mies van der Rohe.

To be clear, in Gestalt terms, we experience the forms of these photographs, paintings, glassware, tables, and chairs, not only because they have structures,

Figure 20 (top left): Josef Albers, *Stacking Tables*, ca. 1927. Ash veneer, black lacquer, and painted glass, 15 5/8 x 16 1/2 x 15 3/4 in. (39.2 x 41.9 x 40 cm); 18 5/8 x 18 7/8 x 15 3/4 in. (47.3 x 48 x 40 cm); 24 5/8 x 23 5/8 x 15 7/8 in. (62.6 x 60.1 x 40.3 cm). The Josef and Anni Albers Foundation (2000.5.3a–d).

Figure 21 (center right): Diagram for motion experiments, Max Werthemer, "Experimentelle Studien über das Sehen von Bewegen," *Zeitschrift für Psychologie* 61 (1912): 262, 264. A translation of the text in this figure is given at note 22.

Figure 22 (bottom left): Josef Albers, *Armchair for Dr. Oeser*, Berlin, 1928. Facsimile reproduction by Jeff Jamieson (2007). Walnut and maplewood veneer, upholstered in Anni Albers's Chenille Stripe fabric by Maharam, 29 1/8 × 24 1/4 × 26 1/2 in. (74 × 61.5 × 67.4 cm). The Josef and Anni Albers Foundation.

but because they *are* structures. We don't just mentally absorb the rhyming forms; they become visual wholes at the moment when we perceive them, and it is our perception that activates them. The shapes that exist in the works of art *also* exist in our perception. They are not established by a binary of images and a representation of those images, but by structural principals that are similar in both the objects *and* our mental processes.

Certainly this kind of "Gestalt seeing" was not the only theoretical resource that influenced Albers's work at the Bauhaus. For example, Kandinsky's book, *Point and Line to Plane*—published as a *Bauhausbücher* in 1926—also explored in some detail the properties of repeating lines and shapes. Indeed, many provocative comparisons can be drawn between the illustrations in Kandinsky's treatise and Albers's art from approximately this time. Furthermore, like the Gestaltists, Kandinsky wrote of the need for a desired unison, or harmony, between what he called the "inner" and "outer" and encouraged an understanding of composition as:

> the internally purposive subordination
> 1. of individual elements
> 2. of the structure [construction] to a concrete pictorial goal.[23]

Yet, Kandinsky always maintained a distinction between the image and the viewer, and relied on sensations to link the object and subject—precisely what the Gestaltists disavowed as too exclusively of the physical world.

Whether or not we accept Gestalt theory as convincing—or Bauhaus theory for that matter—an important takeaway is that by collapsing perception into form, the Gestaltist implied that objects have meanings as well as qualities. In other words, because we cognitively activate form, we give abstract shapes conceptual content. In fact, seeing the Gestalt in art exposes the multiplicities of meaning that are possible in any given perceived object or image. Albers, then, created his designs with an implicit understanding that humans operate with innate mental formulas that determined the way we perceive objects. These are not just abstract shapes and forms. They are, in fact, all content—a fusion of mind and matter.

If we think back to our two parallel institutions—our two parallel lines of the Bauhaus and the Berlin School—and see a correlation there, then it follows that this historical relationality should mean something. These institutions both were complex organizations born of, yet challenging to, the culture of the Weimar Republic. The search for new ways to describe the phenomena of parts and wholes, things and ideas, was surely linked to the traumas and catastrophic changes of the first part of the twentieth century, culminating in World War I and the German Revolution: Rapid industrialization and mechanization; drastic changes to the organization of labor; new forms of communication such as the radio and cinema and the consequent growth of mass audiences. The "crisis in science" that helped propel the Gestalt psychologists was part of the same social and economic equation that caused an upheaval in the realms of art, architecture, photography, and applied design, and which therefore contributed to the creation of institutions like the Bauhaus. As Ash writes, the German psychologists had become immersed in the debates "over matters of the soul in a modernizing society" and this comment could apply just as easily to the artists of the Bauhaus.[24] Gropius's call for a *vielgliedrige Gestalt* in art and architecture, and the Gestaltists's call for unity of mind and matter, were surely both part of a desire for wholeness that stretched across classes, parties, and professions in Weimar Germany, as individuals and institutions searched for a way to make sense of a disrupted world and to redefine what it meant to be human in a country that had been so deeply fractured by violence and upheaval.

Is a Gestalt-inspired history of the Bauhaus possible to construct? If we accept the importance of connected structures, such a history would require a methodology in which everything becomes part of the reconstruction—past, present, evidentiary, archived, recorded *and remembered*. As we have seen, much of the history of Gestalt at the Bauhaus is based on the unscientific data of anecdote and recollection. Furthermore, the premise of Gestalt theory is that the way in which humans perceive material structures must be universal. If all human beings possess innate neural mechanisms that reduce complex images to simpler, more concise forms and consistently see the same patterns and groupings, perceptions are not subjective and cannot be individually or contextually determined. Variations in human perception brought about by ethnicity, geography or chronology—in other words, historical contexts—have no place in those relations between thing and thinking, or between shape and recognition, that characterize Berlin Gestalt at its core. Gestalt theory, therefore, seems to reject its use as a methodology based in temporal analysis, and the Bauhaus as an institution reflective of its moment in time is uneasily examined by Gestalt's universalist eye. However, some experimental psychologists insisted on the inclusion of time in the process. In his critique of the overly objective findings of the Berlin group, Felix Krueger emphasized the importance of feeling and will in our desire to create "cultured wholes."[25] The insistence on generalized characteristics was also complicated by Wertheimer's later studies, in which he explored how perception is influenced by memory practices, and recognized that memory is individualized as well as culturally determined.[26]

Regardless, the abstract, formal properties explored in Bauhaus designs and the psychological universalisms revealed in Gestalt experiments did not change the historical circumstances of the artists and scientists. Both groups were seen as part of a dangerous leftist intelligentsia, and the work of the Bauhaus artists and Gestalt psychologists were viewed with derision as the Weimar Republic moved further and further to the right. The Bauhaus was closed for good shortly after a raid of their temporary quarters in Berlin in 1933, having been shut down by the Nazi party in Dessau the year before. Although it continued to operate under Nazi supervision until 1942, by 1935 Köhler and his associates had been forced out. The Jewish backgrounds of many of the scientists, such as Wertheimer, affected their ability to gain academic posts, publish, and ultimately led to their dismissal and in many cases, emigration. This was also true for Bauhäuslers like Anni Albers, who left Germany for the U.S. in 1933 with her husband Josef.

◙

It is worth looking here at one more documented contact between a Gestaltist and the Bauhaus. In 1927 Rudolf Arnheim visited Dessau to write a review of the Bauhaus building for the journal *Weltbühne*, where he worked as a cultural critic and editor. Trained in Berlin by Köhler and Wertheimer, Arnheim did not go on to practice experimental psychology. Rather, he developed a unique, Gestalt-inspired cultural criticism. Arnheim is mostly known today for his writings on film and art theory, composed after his emigration to the U.S., including two influential texts, *Toward a Psychology of Art* (1949) and *Art and Visual Perception* (1954). In a letter to Roy Behrens many years later, Arnheim dismissed his visit to the Bauhaus as insignificant—"it was summer and nobody, either famous or infamous, was around that I recall."[27] Yet, his essay can offer rich insights into the institutional exchanges that we have been considering.

Arnheim began by setting the Bauhaus building apart from its territory: "Separated by the railway from the thick nest of dusty, peak-roofed, small-town houses and so already isolated in their exterior setting, sit two gigantic, blindingly white blocks…" He went on:

> The will to cleanliness, clarity, and boldness in design has won a victory here…. Every single thing shows its design: no screw is hidden, no decorative carved work to conceal which raw material has been processed there. One is solely tempted to evaluate this honesty also in moral terms.[28]

Arnheim referred to the Bauhaus as a "house of pure function" and described the building in strikingly Gestaltish terms: "a house containing a thousand different things that can be perceived as a structured totality.… Everything depends on how one thing relates to another." The Bauhaus, he wrote, represents a "generally valid psychological phenomenon that leads to very similar results from different people." And, although he did not hesitate to add that the building is perhaps guilty of pretension, he affirms that it is "so good that, for the moment, nothing else is important…. The point is made here more clearly than ever that the practical is really at the same time the beautiful."[29] Arnheim found exactly those kinds of relationships between structures and cognition that emerged from Gestalt experiments in perception: Patterns and structures in the physical substance of the building are perceived by the viewer as a similarly structured totality.

At the same time, two concepts, the moral and the beautiful, distinguish Arnheim's analysis and seem to underscore a different kind of result, one that links these formal properties to something beyond the building itself—to what are surely subjective notions of beauty, while perhaps also signaling the relationship of the Bauhaus to the moral values of his time. Moreover, in one of his first essays published in English, in 1943, Arnheim claimed that the Gestalt approach was simply a scientific "style," analogous to styles in art. He placed the scientific movement in the past, as part of a wave of "romanticism" in Germany—with a "kinship to poets and thinkers of the past, the nearest in time being Goethe."[30] Writing now against the backdrop of yet another world war, Arnheim saw Gestalt psychology as a project of the past—a movement to save the study of perception from rationalism and restore to it a vitality of the human spirit. The reference to Goethe, as a pinnacle of poetic German culture, was surely meant to set him and others like him apart from the brutal repressions of the Nazi regime.

As discussed above, Albers wrote in 1928:

> Adding one element to another element should yield at least one interesting relation that is more than just the sum of those elements. The more variable and intensive the relations that arise, the more valuable the result, the more productive the work.[31]

Not only was Albers describing his own teaching method at the Bauhaus, he was clearly echoing the ideas of Gestalt as he understood them. He was also giving us a prescription for how we might think about these artists, scientists, and thinkers, seen against the backdrop of a troubled moment in history. Precise conclusions might remain elusive—the relationships might be variable—but we learn much about art, history, and science through our comparative efforts.

Notes

1. Josef Albers, "Werklicher Formunterricht," cited in Eeva-Liisa Pelkonen, "Interacting with Albers," *AA Files* 67 (2013), 120. There are two different versions of this essay, translated as "Teaching Form Through Practice." The first, published in *Bauhaus* 2/3 (1928) can be seen in facsimile on the Albers Foundation website, along with a translation by Frederick Amrine, Frederick Horowitz, and Nathan Horowitz, http://albersfoundation.org/teaching/josef-albers/texts/#tab0. Albers published another version three years later in *VI Internationaler Kongress für Zeichne, Kunstunterricht und Angewandte Kunst in Prague, 1928* (Prague, 1931). This later version was included in a special issue on Albers, *AA Files* 67 (2013): 129–131. According to the endnotes, this was a revised version of a translation first published in Hans M. Wingler, *Bauhaus: Weimar, Dessau, Berlin, Chicago* (Cambridge, MA: MIT Press, 1969). Pelkonen references the 1928 original in her essay, and offers some of the sharpest insights into Albers' philosophy; I am deeply indebted not only to the material in her essay, but also its approach. See also: Crétien van Campen, "Early Abstract Art and Experimental Gestalt Psychology" *Leonardo* 30:2 (1997); 133–136; Roy Behrens, "Art Design and Gestalt Theory" *Leonardo* 31:4 (1998); 299–303; Julia Moszkowicz, "Gestalt and Graphic Design: An Exploration of the Humanistic and Therapeutic Effects of Visual Organization," *Design Issues*, 27:4 (Autumn 2011); 56–67; Frederick A. Horowitz and Brenda Danilowitz, *Josef Albers: To Open Eyes: The Bauhaus Black Mountain and Yale* (London: Phaidon, 2006).

2. "Gestalt Theory and Bauhaus—A Correspondence Between Roy Behrens, Brenda Danilowitz, William S. Huff, Lothar Spillmann, Gerhard Temberger and Michael Wertheimer in the Summer of 2011," Introduction and Summary by Geert-Jan Boudewignse, *Gestalt Theory* 34:1 (2012), 81–98.

3. Detlef Mertins, "Hannes Meyer, German Trade Unions School, Bernau 1928–30," in *Bauhaus: Workshops for Modernity, 1919–1933*, eds. Barry Bergdoll and Leah Dickerman (New York: Museum of Modern Art, 2009), 260. Distinctions between the Leipzig group of experimental psychologists and the Berlin group are many. The Leipzig scientists were the first to establish an experimental lab, and their ideas about *Ganzheitspsychologie* (holistic psychology) were closely aligned to that of the Berlin Gestaltists with some important differences. Some Leipzig psychologists, such as Felix Krüger, claimed that their theories of perception predated that of Wertheimer and Köhler—although evidence offered then by the Berlin group and now by historians seems to indicate that the precise workings of Gestalt were clearly established in Berlin, and that the Leipzig group was creating a new mix of their original findings with Gestalt conclusions. See Mitchell G. Ash, *Gestalt Psychology in German Culture, 1890–1967: Holism and the Quest for Objectivity* (Cambridge, U.K.: Cambridge University Press, 1995), esp. chap. 18.

4. Hannes Beckmann, "Formative Years," in *Bauhaus and Bauhaus People*, ed. Eckhard Neumann, 2nd ed. (New York: Van Nostrand Rheinhold, 1993 [1970]), 209.

5. Ash, *Gestalt Psychology in German Culture*, esp. 245, 260; Marianne Teuber, "Blue Knight by Paul Klee" in *Vision and Artifact: Essays in Honor of Rudolf Arnheim*, ed. M. Henle (New York: Springer, 1976), 149; Marianne Teuber, *Paul Klee: Paintings and Watercolors from the Bauhaus Years, 1921–1931* (Des Moines, IA: Art Center, 1973), 6–17. See also D. Brett King

and Michael Wertheimer, *Max Wertheimer and Gestalt Theory* (New Brunswick, NJ: Transaction, 2005), 157–58.

6. See, for example, Rainer Wick, *Teaching at the Bauhaus* (Ostvildern-Ruit: Hatje Cantz Verlag, 2000), 200, 220, 240; Paul Overy, *Kandinsky: The Language of the Eye* (New York: Praeger, 1970).

7. "Architekten, Maler und Bildhauser müssen die vielgliedrige Gestalt des Baues in seiner Gesamtheit und in seinen Teilen wieder kennen lernen…." Walter Gropius, "Program of the Staatliche Bauhaus in Weimar," in Hans Wingler, *Bauhaus: Weimar Dessau Berlin Chicago* (Cambridge, MA: MIT Press, 1984), 31. The Wingler collection of primary documents, translated by Wolfgang Jabs and Bail Gilbert, uses the phrase "composite character," as does Frank Whitford in *The Bauhaus: Masters and Students by Themselves* (New York: Overlook, 1993), 38. Peter Gay, however, translates this important phase as "the multiform shape" in *Weimar Culture: The Outsider as Insider* (New York: Harper and Rowe, 1980), 98; quoted in Wertheimer, 158.

8. T. Lux Feininger, "The Bauhaus: Evolution of an Idea," in *Bauhaus and Bauhaus People*, 183.

9. Wingler, *Bauhaus: Weimar Dessau Berlin Chicago*, 32–33.

10. For a recent discussion of this debate, see *German Art History and Scientific Thought: Beyond Formalism*, ed. Mitchell B. Frank and Daniel Adler (Surrey: Ashgate, 2012).

11. *Bauhaus Reviewed 1919–1933* (sound recording) (London: LTM, 2007); Albers was recorded in 1968 by George Baird. Albers refers to an exchange with a psychologist named "Krueger," perhaps in reference to Felix Krueger of the Leipzig experimental psychology laboratory. This would offer further evidence of a connection between the Dessau Bauhaus and Karlfried Graf von Dürkheim from the Leipzig group who visited in 1930–31. For a non-specialist discussion of the Berlin group, and its differentiation from the Leipzig psychologists, see Johan Wagemans, James H. Elder, Michael Kobovy, Stephen E. Palmer, Mary A. Peterson, Manish Singh, and Rüdiger von der Heydt, "A Century of Gestalt Psychology in Visual Perception," in *Psychology Bulletin* 139:6 (November 2012), 1172–1217. Published online July 30, 2012 at http://www.ncbi.nlm.nih.gov/pmc/articles/PMC3482144/, accessed May 1, 2015.

12. For this essay I have drawn principally upon the exceptional social and intellectual history of Gestalt in Mitchell G. Ash, *Gestalt Psychology in German Culture, 1890–1967: Holism and the Quest for Objectivity* (Cambridge: Cambridge University Press, 1995).

13. See John V. Maciuika, *Before the Bauhaus: Architecture, Politics and the German State, 1890-1920* (Cambridge: Cambridge University Press, 2008).

14. Joseph Ben David and Randall Collins, "Social Factors in the Origins of a New Science: The Case of Psychology," *American Sociological Review* 31 (1966): 45. Although he mentions that the study is oft-cited, Ash gives evidence that this hybridization was institutionally problematic, and does not support the conclusion that this mixing of disciplines led to explosive growth, as do David and Collins. See Ash, *Gestalt Psychology in German Culture*, 17.

15. See Ash, *Gestalt Psychology in German Culture*, Introduction and Chapter 20. For a recent discussion of the complicated history of the Bauhaus and National Socialism, see Paul Jaskot, "The Nazi Party's Strategic use of the Bauhaus" in *Renew Marxist Art History*, ed. Warren Carter, Barnaby Haran and Frederic Schwartz (London: Art Books, 2013), 382–399.

16. Among the earliest revisionist histories are Magdalena Droste's *Bauhaus: 1919–1933* (Köln: Taschen, 1990); *Bauhaus Weimar: Designs for the Future*, ed. by Michael Siebenbrodt and

Elisabeth Reissinger (Ostfildern-Ruit: Hatje Cantz Publishers, 2000); and *Bauhaus*, ed. by Jeanine Fiedler and Peter Feierabend (Cologne: Könemann, 1999). Winfred Nerdinger's *Bauhaus Moderne im Nationalsozialismus* (Munich: Prestel, 1993), and Barbara Miller Lane's *Architecture and Politics in Germany, 1918–1945* (Cambridge, MA: Harvard University Press, 1985), attested to the complicated political history of the Bauhaus. More recently, the catalogues from the exhibitions in Berlin and New York, *Bauhaus: A Conceptual Model* (Ostfildern: Hatje Cantz, 2009), and *Bauhaus: Workshops for Modernity*, ed. by Barry Bergdoll and Leah Dickerman (New York: The Museum of Modern Art, 2009), presented exhaustive analyses of the work of the school, and should be consulted for a full list of sources on the Bauhaus, including the work of Josef Albers. The catalogue of the London exhibition, *Bauhaus: Art as Life*, by Kathleen James-Chakraborty, Eva Forgacs, Ayna Baumhoff and Klaus Weber, contributed to these expanded views. Other important essay collections include: *Bauhaus Construct: Fashioning Identity, Discourse and Modernism*, ed. by Jeffrey Saletnik and Robin Schuldenfrei (London: Routledge, 2009); *Bauhaus Conflicts 1919-2009: Controversies and Counterparts*, ed. by Phillipp Oswalt (Ostfildern: Hatje Cantz, 2010); and *Bauhaus Culture: From Weimar to the Cold War*, ed. by Kathleen James-Chakraborty (Minneapolis: University of Minnesota Press, 2006). It has always been the contention of this author that there was not one, but many "Bauhauses"; see Karen Koehler, "Which Bauhaus?" in *Centropa*, 3:1 (January 2003); 79–80; "The Bauhaus: A Conceptual Model," *Journal of the Society of Architectural Historians*, 69:1 (March 2010); 434–436; *Bauhaus Modern* (Northampton, MA: Smith College Museum of Art, 2008); and "The Bauhaus Manifesto Postwar to Postwar" in *Bauhaus Constructs*, 2009, op. cit.

17. See, for example, *Gestalt Therapy: History, Theory and Practice*, ed. by Ansel Woldt and Sarah M. Toman (London: Sage Publishers, 2005).

18. For a brilliant and detailed discussion of how Gestalt fits into the complex web of German art historiography, see Frederic J. Schwartz, *Blind Spots: Critical Theory and the History of Art in Twentieth Century Germany* (New Haven: Yale University Press, 2005), 161–162.

19. Ash, *Gestalt Psychology in German Culture*, 1 (italics his).

20. We also know that Albers had books on psychology in his personal library in Connecticut in the 1950s (including, for example, Bruno Petermann, *Das Gestaltproblem in der Psychologie* (Leipzig: Verlag von Johann Abrosius Barth, 1931)—although exactly when and how he came to own these books is unknown.

21. The German text in this excerpt from Wertheimer's article reads as follows:

    6. In all cases under discussion, a first simple principle can be seen: Dots separated by small distances group naturally. Perceptual grouping of dots with large separations does not arise, or does so only with great effort, and is less stable. In a provisional formulation: All else being equal, perceptual grouping tends to form more easily across smaller separations. (Factor of proximity.)

    This is a most general and ubiquitous principle of perceptual grouping, and is not confined to visual grouping, nor even spatial experience. Continuous tapping of rhythms, for instance in the pattern of series 1 (etc.), or in the pattern of series 2d (etc.) show the effect in a most definite way....

    8. Present a configuration of equidistant dots in pairs of different color on a homogeneous field: for instance, white and black in a gray field, in the schema: (8a). Or, better, fill a surface with this schema: (8b, 8c). Or 8d...

One generally sees the grouping in which similar elements group with each other: in 8a, ab/cd...; in 8b, the verticals; in 8c, the horizontals; in 8d, abc/def....

It is generally impossible to get the alternative grouping to appear simultaneously and clearly across the whole pattern: in 8a, .../bc/de/...; in 8b, the horizontals; in 8c, the verticals; in 8d, any of the groupings cde/fgh...or the like.

For this, and translations and discussion of the both the 1923 and 1912 studies (below at note 22), see Max Wertheimer, *On Perceived Motion and Figural Organization*, ed. Lothar Spillmann with contributions by Michael Wertheimer, K.W. Watkins, Steven Lehar, Robert Sekuler, Viktor Sarris, and Lothar Spillman (Cambridge, MA: MIT Press, 2012).

22. The German text in this excerpt from Wertheimer's article reads as follows:

In the visual field (within the motion field or outside it), a third object c is presented in one of the two exposure fields, or identically in both. For variations, see §10.

Wertheimer, *On Perceived Motion and Figural Organization*, 90.

23. Wassily Kandinsky, "Point and Line to Plane" in *Kandinsky: Complete Works on Art*, Vol. 2, eds. Kenneth Lindsay and Peter Vergo (Boston: G.K. Hall, 1982), 552, 614, passim.

24. Ash, *Gestalt Psychology in German Culture*, 205.

25. Felix Krueger, *Über Entwickungspsychologie* (Jena, 1915), discussed in Ash, *Gestalt Psychology in German Culture*, 311–312, and mentioned by Albers in 1968 (see note 11).

26. Max Wertheimer left Berlin in 1929 to establish a Gestalt program at the University of Frankfurt, and his proximity to Karl Manheim at the University and Max Horkheimer at the Frankfurt School for Social Research brought students and faculty together in both courses and shared facilities. Although outside of the scope of this essay, further explorations of tripartite connections among the Frankfurtschule theories of culture and social relations, Gestalt theories of perception, and Bauhaus theories of art and architecture will surely expand the way this history can be told; see Ash, *Gestalt Psychology in German Culture*, 215; and, more generally, Schwarz, *Blind Spots*.

27. "Gestalt Theory and Bauhaus—A Correspondence" in *Gestalt Theory* 34:1 (2012), 90.

28. Rudolf Arnheim, "The Bauhaus in Dessau" in *Weimar Republic Sourcebook*, ed. by Anton Kaes, Martin Jay, and Edward Dimendberg (Berkeley: University of California Press, 1994), 450 (originally published as "Das Bauhaus in Dessau," *Die Weltbuhne* 23:22 (May 31, 1927), 920–921). For a discussion of Arnheim's role as a cultural critic in Weimar Germany—as well as the political position of the journal, see Dirk Grathoff, "Rudolf Arnheim at the Weltbuhne" in *Rudolf Arnheim: Revealing Vision*, ed. by Kent Kleinman and Leslie Van Duzer (Ann Arbor: University of Michigan Press), 1997; 18–25.

29. Arnheim, "The Bauhaus in Dessau," 451.

30. Rudolf Arnheim, "Gestalt and Art," *Journal of Aesthetics and Art Criticism* 2:8 (Fall 1943), 70.

31. Josef Albers, "Teaching Form Through Practice," *AA Files* 67 (2013), 129.

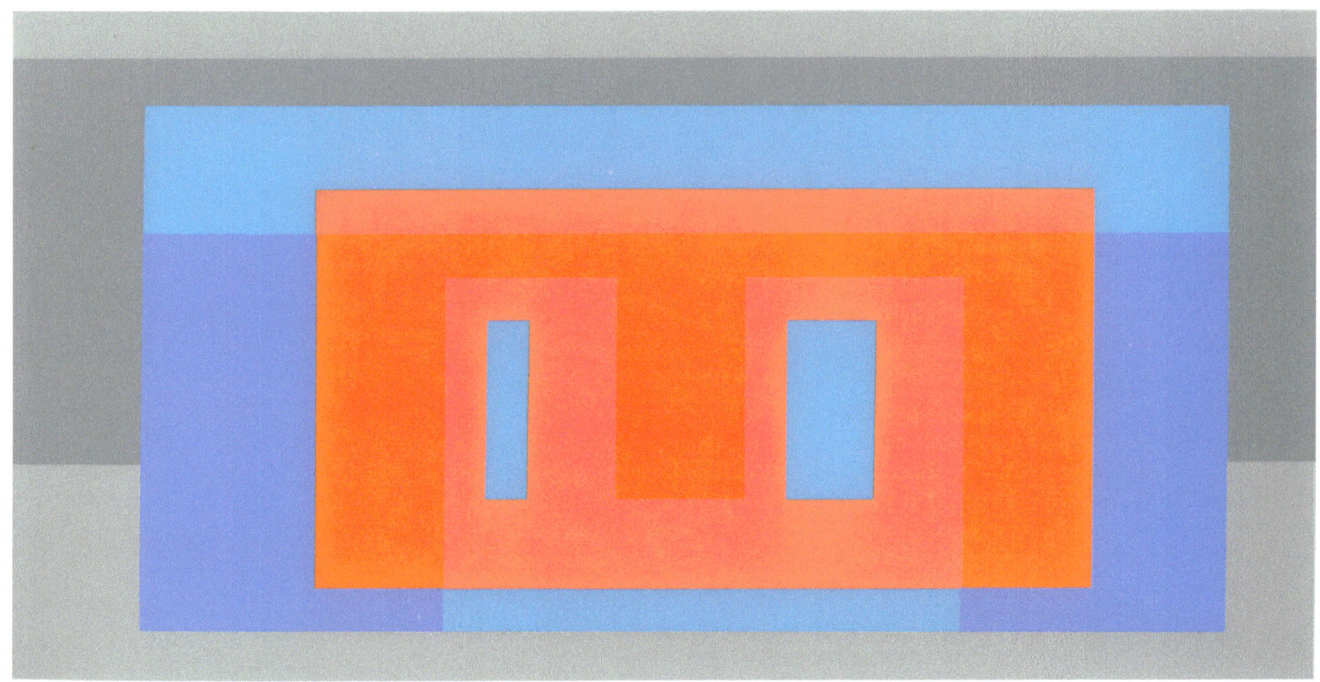

Cat. 17: Josef Albers, *Formulation : Articulation*, Folio I / Folder 17 ["Variants II"], 1972. Screenprint, 15 x 20 in. (38.1 x 50.8 cm). Mead Art Museum, Amherst College, gift of the Alan M. Sternlieb Study Collection (1979.103.1.17.b).

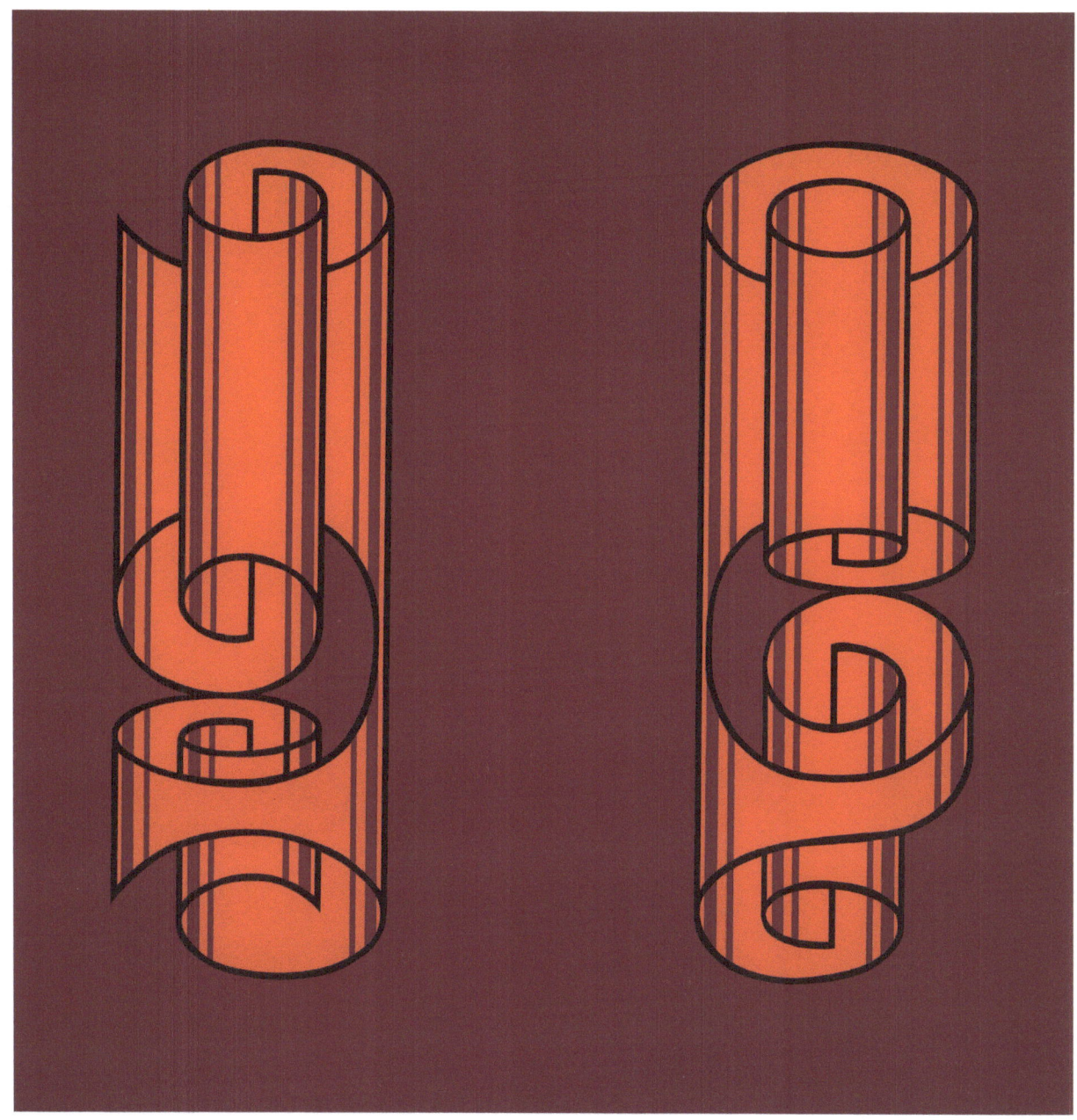

Cat. 18: Josef Albers, *Formulation : Articulation*, Folio I / Folder 18 ["Rolled Wrongly"], 1972. Screenprint, 15 x 20 in. (38.1 x 50.8 cm). Mead Art Museum, Amherst College, gift of the Alan M. Sternlieb Study Collection (1979.103.1.18.b).

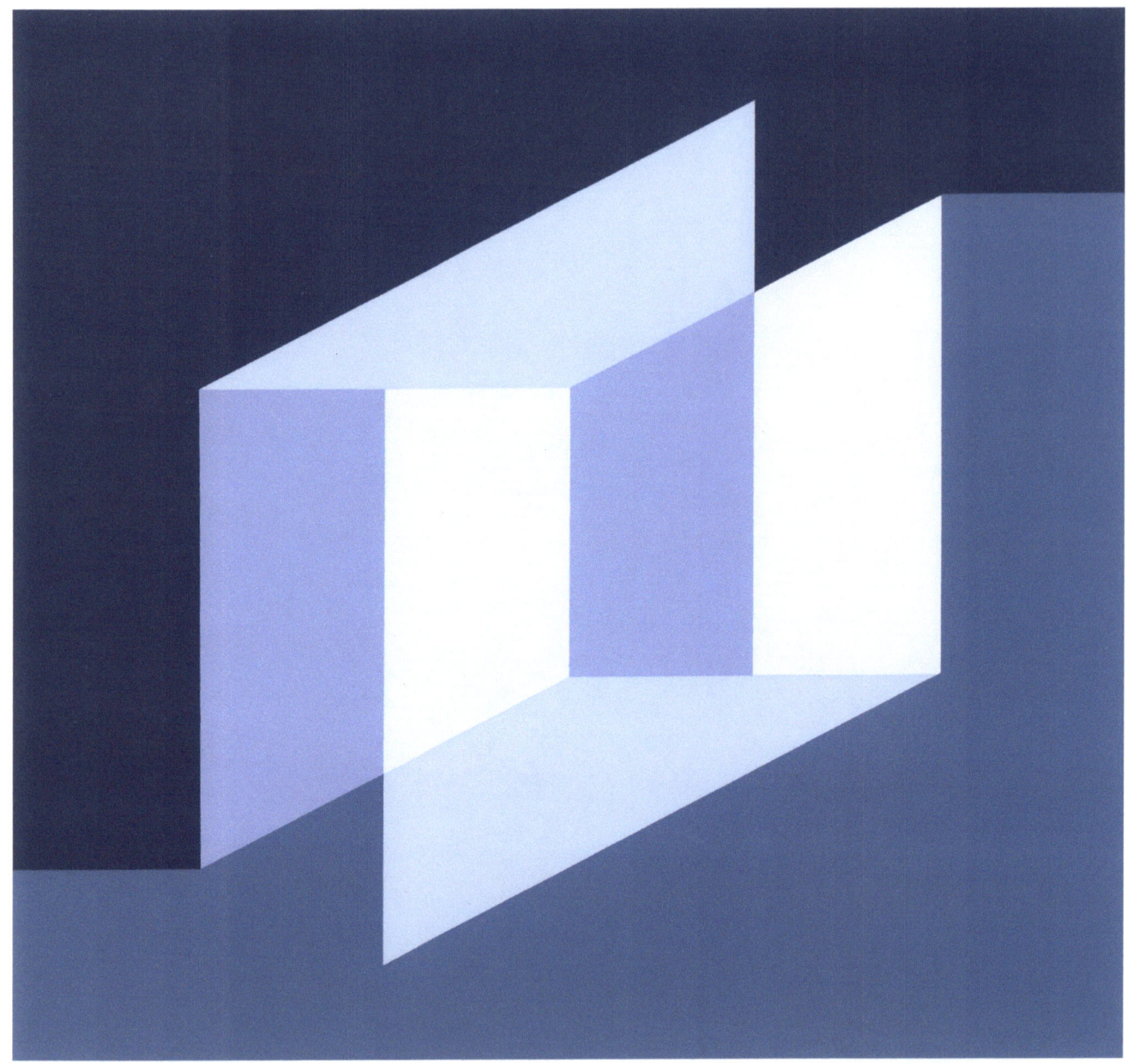

Cat. 28: Josef Albers, *Formulation : Articulation*, Folio II / Folder 25, 1972. Screenprint, 15 x 20 in. (38.1 x 50.8 cm). Mead Art Museum, Amherst College, gift of the Alan M. Sternlieb Study Collection (1979.103.2.25.b).

Juxtapositions and Constellations: Albers and Op Art

Jeffrey Saletnik

In 1971 Josef Albers wrote to the philosopher and art historian Cyril Barrett in response to the publication of Barrett's book *Op Art*, a 191-page critical survey of the optical effects employed by artists associated with the genre.[1] "Seeing again, how unimportant you have treated me [*sic*] in your 'Op Art,'" he wrote, "particularly in chapters 7 and 8, I feel obliged to send you enclosed an article of the Oct. 15 issue of 'Vogue' magazine...."[2] Barrett's almost complete omission of Albers from the chapters titled "Principal figures in the European movement" and "British and American Op" represented, to Albers, yet another tacit dismissal of his work: hence his need to point out the author's seeming oversight. Much of the article he sent to Barrett, Sam Hunter's "Josef Albers: 'Prophet and Presiding Genius of American OP Art,'" detailed the artist's difficulty in finding acceptance among the aesthetic trends of his adopted country and his self-understanding as having been "the black sheep" among such American avant-garde artists of the 1940s and 1950s as Jackson Pollock, Willem de Kooning, and Franz Kline.[3] Indeed, Albers had garnered less critical attention than those aligned with so-called Painterly Abstraction. However, as the *Vogue* article's reverential title indicates, by 1970 Hunter—as well as the curator William C. Seitz, who praised Albers as a "master of perceptual abstraction"—had recognized how the artist's work modeled the perceptual practices for which painters such as Richard Anuszkiewicz and Julian Stanczak were known.[4] And although the "master" disliked the term itself, op art represented an apotheosis of painting to Albers, who claimed that "only when our minds are directed through appropriate juxtapositions (combination[s]) and constellations (placements) of color and shape will we sense their relatedness and mutual actions; then *to see* art will become a creative act."[5]

Unfortunately, for Albers, Hunter and Seitz held a minority opinion at the time; the relevance of Albers's interest in perception did not resonate with parallel problems being pursued in postwar American painting, a situation that Albers and his proponents were unable to circumvent. Many artists affiliated with op art were derided for their emphasis on psychophysical effects and for the association of their work with fashion. (Albers's choice to send Barrett a copy of an essay published in *Vogue*, albeit one written by a highly regarded art historian and curator, was somewhat ironic.) And many critics were unable to disassociate Albers from the Bauhaus and problems of painting related to an early twentieth-century European tradition. (Barrett actually didn't consider Albers's work to be op art: "[Albers] is usually classed among the Op artists, yet many, if not most, of his paintings are not Op at all—certainly not 'hard core' Op."[6]) As the discrepancy between the views of Hunter and Barrett indicate, scholars and critics found it difficult to classify Albers's work, or even to consider it under the umbrella of op art—an association the artist himself embraced.[7] This essay explores Albers's relationship to American art critical discourse on painting in the 1960s, exposing the tenuous position of his work and ideas therein. Ultimately, it posits a relationship between Albers and Robert Irwin's dematerialized paintings and installations, the latter being an extension of Albers's aesthetic but unencumbered by traditions of painting and thus able to realize Albers's vision more completely.

In the mid-1960s, the positioning of a painter's work in relation to the rapidly changing understanding of the artist–object–viewer nexus would prove crucial as discursive trends developed. The terms of this discourse were elaborated in a number of important exhibitions. Along with Clement Greenberg's 1964 exhibition "Post Painterly Abstraction" at the Los Angeles County Museum of Art, and Lawrence Alloway's "Systemic Painting" exhibition at the Guggenheim Museum in 1966, "The Responsive Eye," held at the Museum of Modern Art in 1965, helped establish the stakes of abstract painting in the wake of Abstract Expressionism and in opposition to pop art. Although there was significant overlap among artists included in these exhibitions (Ellsworth Kelly, Thomas Downing, Kenneth Noland, and Frank Stella were shown in each), the critical frameworks in which the respective exhibitions operated differed significantly.[8]

Seitz, who curated "The Responsive Eye" and objected to the term "op art," cast the objects included in the exhibition as devices that affect viewer perception and thereby viewer psychology.[9] Their historical significance was measured by their relation to a tradition of art-making informed by physiological and psychological understandings of perception developed since the late nineteenth century, yet the exhibited works also engaged issues relevant to contemporary aesthetics. In Seitz's view, the lack of personal marks on the surfaces of the works, as well as the materials out of which many were made, constituted a visual economy that drew attention away from artistic subjectivity and/or the objects' form, and toward the perceptual—and psychophysical—response of the viewers: some found the show literally nauseating. This ran counter to Greenberg's assertion that work from some of the very same artists indicated an evolution from Painterly Abstraction (which, to Greenberg, had become an aesthetic habit by the 1960s) to Post Painterly Abstraction—work that favored "openness of design," "linear clarity," and "contrasts of pure hue."[10] These recent formal trends constituted a style in keeping with the modernist ontology of painting as hermetic and bound to the essential flatness of the painting surface.[11] They also emphasized opticality as the primary condition of painting.[12] Whereas Seitz prioritized viewer response and Greenberg pointed out how aspects of recent work corresponded to the integral nature of painting, Alloway was interested in the artist as conceiver of the "syntax" for his or her painting. In the essay that accompanied his "Systemic Painting" exhibition, Alloway stressed that one ought to attend to the organization of a painting as the result of an artist's human effort —its system, which could "occur off the canvas"—and thereby view it as both a personal and a "factual display" rather than merely as a work that exists in service of aesthetic ideals.[13]

Works by Albers, Anuszkiewicz, and Stanczak were included only in "The Responsive Eye," thus indicating their positioning relative to this discourse: To invoke Albers's terminology, their work engaged the dialectic between the "physical fact" of the object and its "psychic effect" upon the viewer. Greenberg, who like most critics associated Albers with the Bauhaus and thereby with practices that predated Painterly Abstraction, made clear how the formal linearity he observed in Post Painterly Abstract painting was a response to the painterly aspects of the style's immediate predecessor (Painterly Abstraction) rather than a reintroduction of the geometries associated with "Mondrian, the Bauhaus, Suprematism, or anything that came before."[14] Whereas Albers's painting and Greenberg's vision were formally incompatible, one might argue that Albers's *Homage to the Square* series in fact suited Alloway's criteria.[15] Certainly, Albers's repetitive use of nested squares of color over a sixteen-year period by the time of Alloway's exhibition amounted to an artist-generated syntax based upon a module, "the run of [which] constitutes a system,…which we learn empirically by seeing enough of the work."[16] His *Homage to the Square* series was by no means conceptual art, but Alloway and others—including Albers himself—largely overlooked its significance as part of a sustained practice. Rather, for Albers, each of his paintings maintained its individuality insofar as each work "proclaim[ed] color autonomy as a means of plastic organization" differently and originally.[17]

And so the paintings were received, at times, to mixed reviews. In 1964 Donald Judd described even Albers's "first rate" paintings as "pat" and "predictable."[18] Barbara Rose, in contrast, noted how Albers's work sought to bring color and structure into relationship with each other, thus engaging the "two main currents" of twentieth-century art initiated by Matisse and Picasso, respectively.[19] It was with these artists, along with Kandinsky, that she placed Albers. In her review of "The Responsive Eye" she singled out the work of Albers, Ad Reinhardt, and others in the exhibition as "art of the highest order" in which perceptual effect "[did] not constitute the *entire* content of the work."[20] But in doing so, she disassociated Albers from op art, and went along with critics who found that his work resonated with problems of painting posited at the beginning of the twentieth century rather than contemporary trends. Like the majority of the art critical establishment, she condemned "The Responsive Eye" and, by extension, op art. It lacked "expressive content," she claimed; op art was "sensational" and "hip"; its artists traded in optical trickery to elicit immediate, visceral responses from viewers. Op art, she added, was "decorative," "easily-experienced," and designed to satisfy an "appetite for popular entertainment"—comments that were intended to evoke long-standing anxieties about modernity.

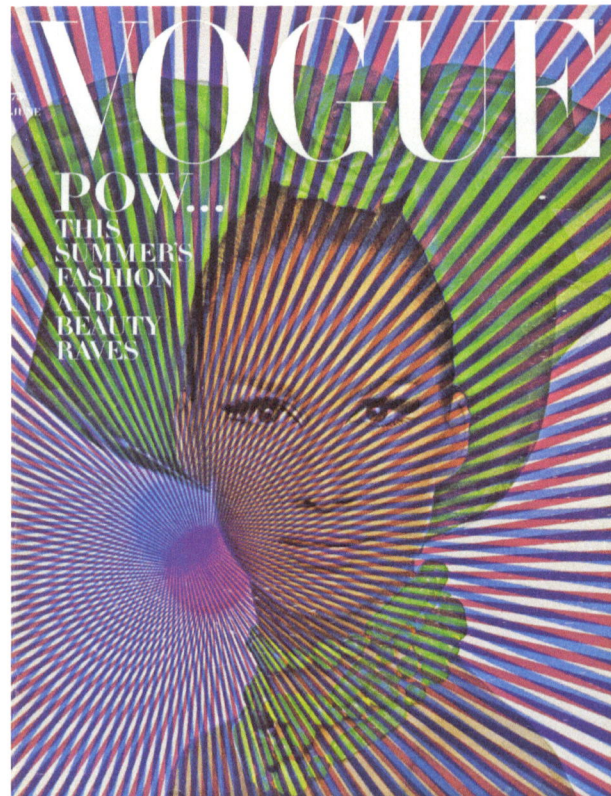

Figure 23: Cover, *Vogue* (U.S.), June 1965. Montage with photograph by Irene Penn and serigraph construction by Gerald Oster.

Indeed, if not actually a byproduct of modernity, op art seemed to have a complacent relationship with modernity that was troubling; Alloway, for example, noted how the conditions that gave rise to its appeal challenged the authority of critics writing for "specialized journals."[21] In an issue of *Vogue* (U.S.) published in the same year (1970) as Hunter's laudatory article about Albers, one found a lavishly illustrated article devoted to an "op-art-ment" designed by François Catroux. Notably, in June of 1965 the magazine's U.S. cover had featured an image of a model's face overlaid with moiré patterns by Gerald Oster (fig. 23).[22] In April of 1965 *Life* magazine featured the high-end textiles that Larry Aldrich famously—and controversially—based on paintings by Bridget Riley and other artists.[23] Rather than entering the discourse and popular consciousness after having been vetted by art critics and historians, op art found its admirers—and established its value—in popular magazines, leaving serious art critics, according to Alloway, little choice in their response other than disdain.

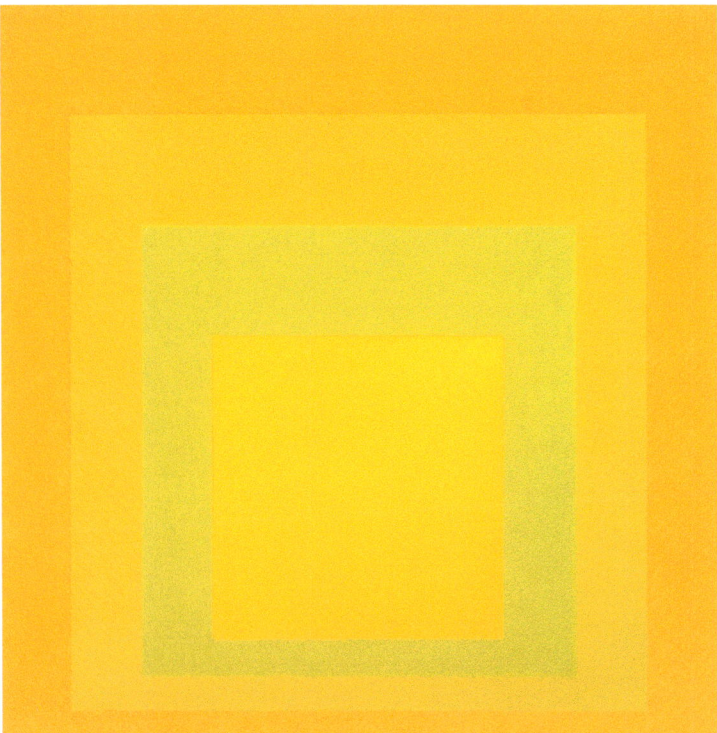
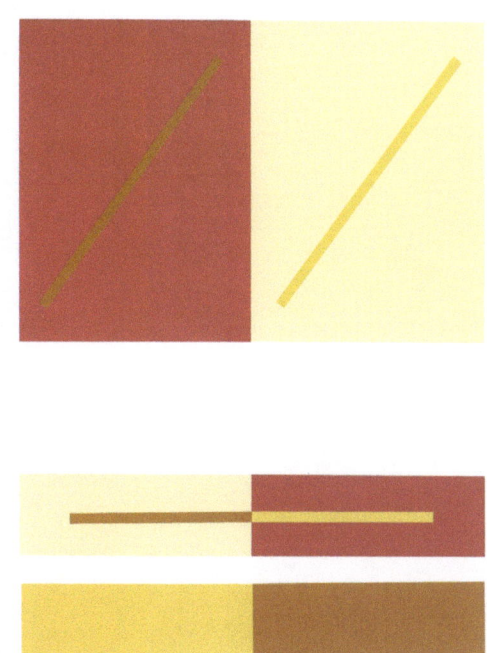

Despite being met with disapproval by most art critics, op art's prominence confirmed the currency of Albers's unyielding belief that art existed in a state of tension between "physical fact and psychic effect."[24] It also encouraged his long-held interest in Gestalt psychology (explored in Karen Koehler's contribution to this volume) and Rudolf Arnheim, and his desire that those viewing his canvases regard the activity of seeing as itself a creative act. For Albers, op art—or his preferred descriptor, "perceptual art"—brought the dynamic functioning of the medium of color to the fore of discourse on painting. Indeed, the demonstration of color's relativity had been a central tenet of his painting practice and color instruction, which was published as *Interaction of Color* in 1963.[25]

One can see, for example, how color dynamics are essential to his *Homage to the Square: Wondering* (fig. 24), which was shown in "The Responsive Eye." Upon prolonged viewing it becomes apparent how the four nested squares of unmixed color are held in visual tension with one another. The deep cadmium yellow along the outer edge of the painting and the innermost light cadmium yellow square remain stable, holding the interstitial deep and light Naples yellow squares in place as they register degrees of chartreuse in competition with one another to assert chromatic dominance.[26] Of course, the pigments that Albers

Figure 24 (left): Josef Albers, *Homage to the Square: Wondering*, 1964. Oil on Masonite, 48 x 48 in. (121.9 x 121.9 cm). Saint Louis Art Museum, bequest of John M. and Eleanor S. Shoenberg (29:1997). Image courtesy Saint Louis Art Museum.

Figure 25 (right): Josef Albers, Plate VII-5b from *Interaction of Color*, Yale University Press (1963). Image courtesy the Josef and Anni Albers Foundation/Yale University Press.

Juxtapositions and Constellations: Josef Albers and Op Art

Figure 26: Richard J. Anuszkiewicz, *The Sounding of the Bell*, 1964. Polymer on Masonite, 48 x 48 in. (121.9 x 121.9 cm). Yale University Art Gallery (1964.16). © Richard Anuszkiewicz.

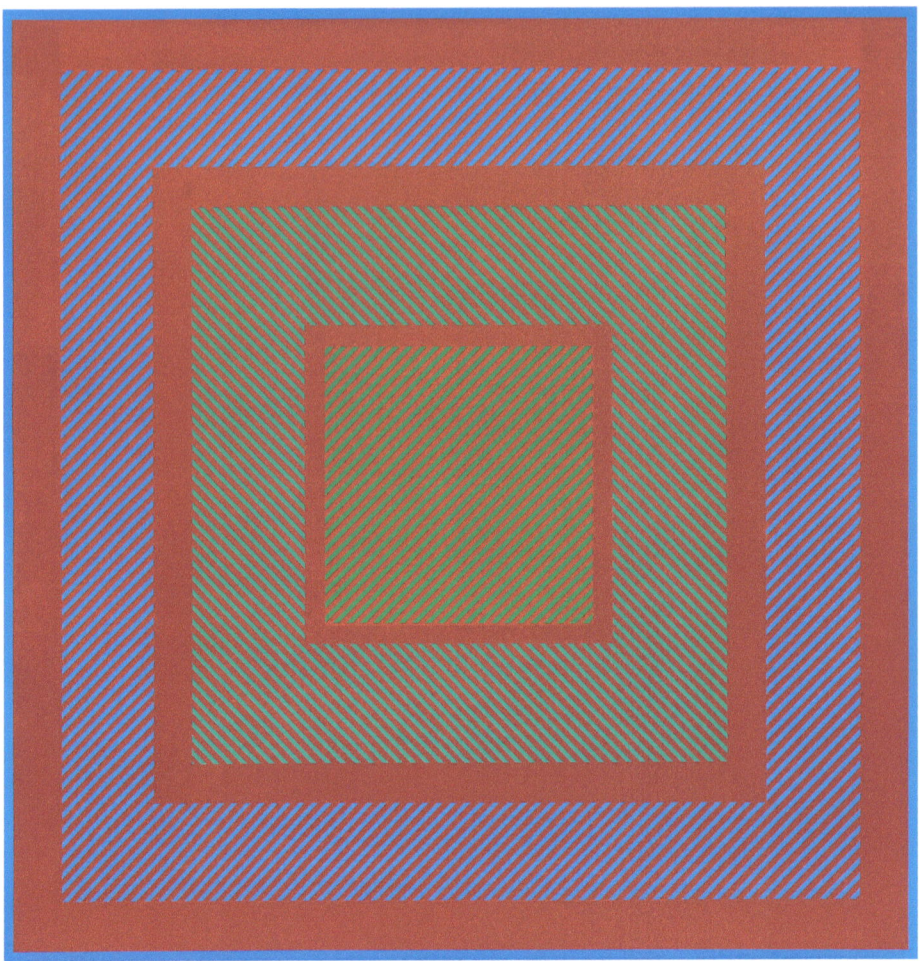

applied to the surface directly from the manufacturer's tubes are materially fixed; that they appear to shift hues despite our knowing this detail is the point, insofar as Albers draws our attention to the picture plane as an unresolvable situation. The crafting of such images was key to the color studies he asked students to complete.

For example, Plate VII-5b from *Interaction of Color* (fig. 25) shows how the ground upon which a color is placed can radically affect the way in which it is perceived. In the uppermost pair of rectangles, the diagonal stripes (from left to right) are ochre and Naples yellow, but they appear to be nearly the same hue when placed, respectively, upon deep red and off-white grounds. (The "factual" colors are indicated in the lowermost rectangles on the page.) By exchanging the ground colors the image draws attention to the relativity of color perception, bringing the stripes closer to, yet still not in perfect consonance with, their "factual" hues.

Richard Anuszkiewicz, who studied with Albers between 1953 and 1955 and is commonly associated with op art, used the lessons of Albers's instruction as the basis of his own painting practice. In *The Sounding of the Bell* (fig. 26) he exploits the optical effect of adding color to the picture plane in precisely measured parallel lines. These lines, juxtaposed with the painting's red ground, create the presence of colors not materially present on the surface while also mining perspectival conventions to create the appearance of depth and projection simultaneously. Rosalind Krauss, extending Greenberg's prioritization of painting as a purely optical art, wrote that op art actually was "compulsive[ly] illusionist" and based upon the crafting of *"trompe l'oeil* tactility;" it didn't matter, as in Anuszkiewicz's work, that dimensionality was "calculated to occur on the retina" rather than upon painted surfaces themselves. Singling out Anuszkiewicz's contribution to "The Responsive Eye," she wrote that the "picture's structure…depends not on color as a primary sensation but on its incidental properties for evoking value contrasts: the result is a work centered on a tactile mode…."[27] Albeit an impressive manifestation of Albers's aesthetic priorities, a work like *The Sounding of the Bell* ultimately could not evade the medium-specific concerns of discourse on painting.

Although op art was not aligned with dominant American discourse on abstract painting set forth by the likes of Greenberg, Alloway, and Krauss, it corresponded to a nascent practice in which perception itself was employed as an artist's medium. By the end of the 1960s Robert Irwin, who was among the artists included in "The Responsive Eye," had pushed painting beyond the limitations of its material parameters in crafting work, as in his disc paintings, which blurred the boundaries between the painted object and the space surrounding it.[28] In 1970 he altered the fluorescent lighting scheme of an empty gallery in the Museum of Modern Art and suspended a translucent scrim at the midpoint and four feet from the ceiling, thereby creating, in a work known as "the room at the Museum of Modern Art," three zones of light intensity: above the scrim (and closest to the light source), as diffused by the scrim, and below the scrim. One's ability to perceive the otherwise empty white-walled space constituted the work of art; as Irwin noted, "everything in the installation conspired to skew one's expectations,…so that your perceptual mechanism became tilted, and you perceived the room as you otherwise might not have."[29] It is as though Irwin expanded into three dimensions Albers's practice of employing color and form to compose a painting based on unresolvable visual dissonance. In doing so, he asked those who experienced his work to grapple with their "being and circum-

Figure 27: Robert Irwin, *Excursus: Homage to the Square³*, Dia Center for the Arts, 548 West 22nd Street, New York City, September 13, 1998-June 13, 1999. © Robert Irwin/Artists Rights Society (ARS), New York. Photo: Thibault Jeanson. Image courtesy the Dia Art Foundation, New York.

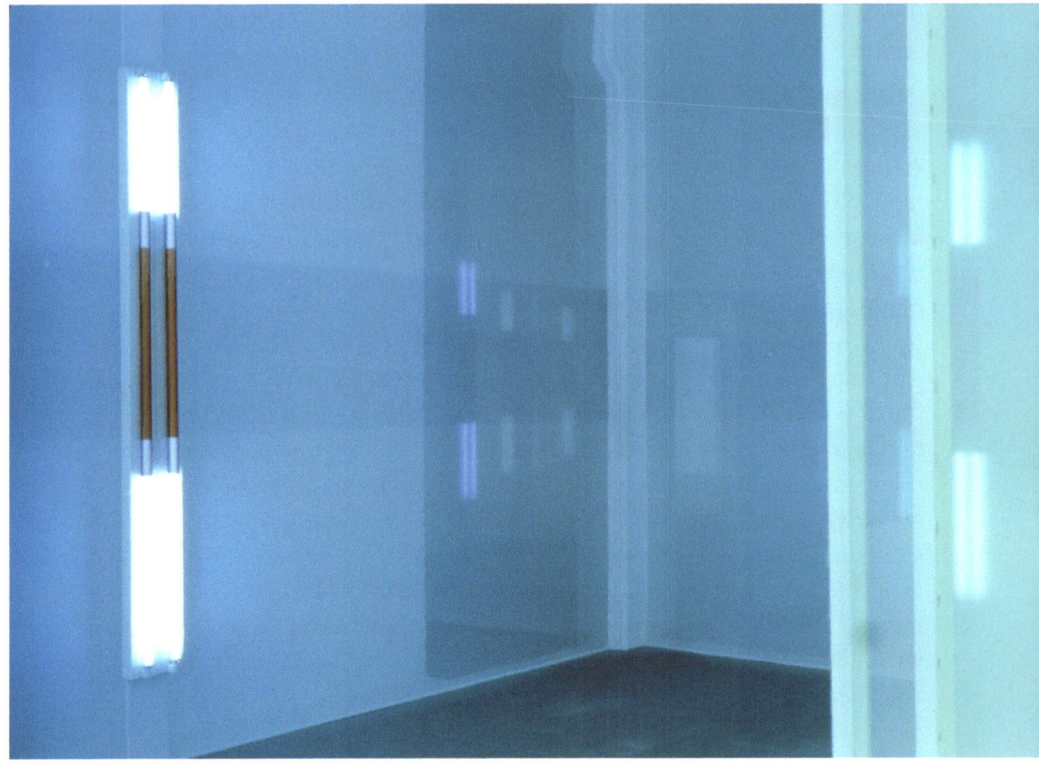

stance," with coming to understand all perception as embodied, conditioned, circumstantial, and, to invoke Albers, as a creative act.[30]

Irwin's *Excursus: Homage to the Square³* (fig. 27) made this explicit. The installation, according to Irwin, "approach[ed] color as a kind of infinite possibility, as Albers did," yet in lived space.[31] For the first showing of the work, originally conceived for the Dia Center for the Arts exhibition space in New York City (now named Dia:Chelsea), Irwin used a floor-to-ceiling translucent scrim to divide one floor of the building into a double-walled grid of eighteen interconnected rooms of equal size. He mounted two vertical fluorescent light fixtures at the midpoint of walls throughout the space, covering the midsections of these fixtures with differently colored theatrical gels. As one wandered from room to room, the delicate mixture of colored light shifted subtly, while the silhouettes of bodies elsewhere in the installation registered with varying degrees of clarity though layers of scrim and light, all of which made the viewer aware of him- or herself as but one of several shadowy forms moving in space. Thus, in unbinding his thinking from problems of painting and the making of discrete

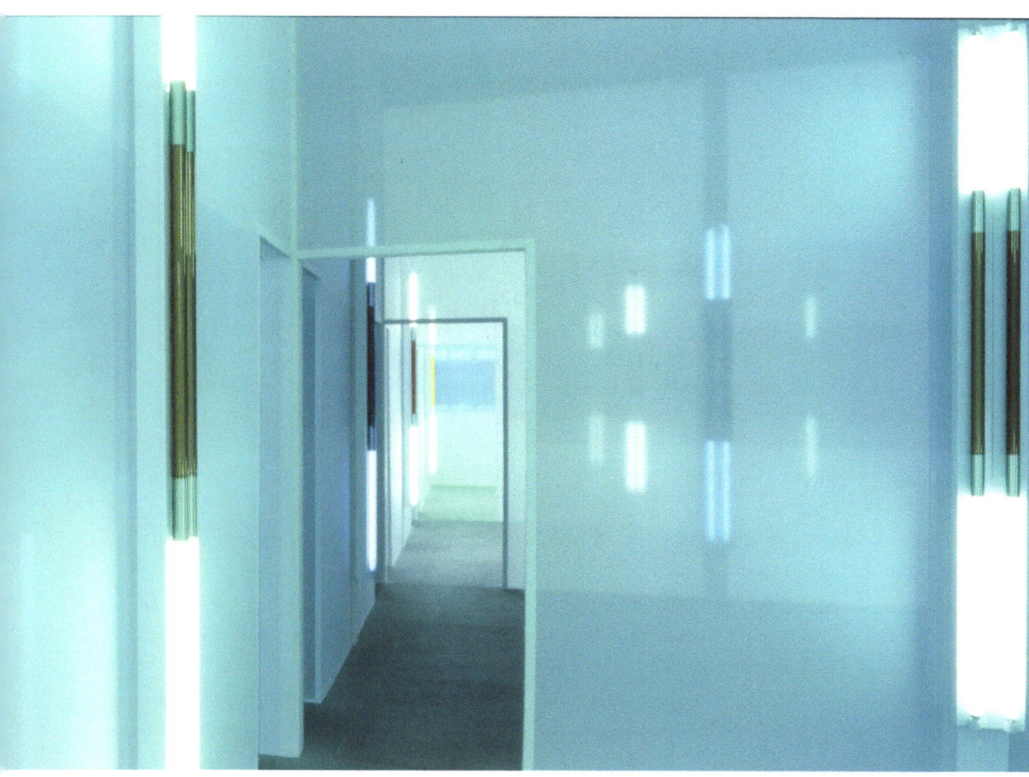

objects—as Albers, his critics, and Anuszkiewicz seemed unable to do—Irwin brought the lessons of Albers's perceptual practice to light.

Notes

1. Cyril Barrett, *Op Art* (New York: Viking Press, 1970).
2. Josef Albers to Cyril Barrett, July 28, 1971. The Josef and Anni Albers Foundation, Bethany, Connecticut.
3. See Sam Hunter, "Josef Albers: 'Prophet and Presiding Genius of American OP Art,'" *Vogue* (U.S.), October 1970, 70–73, 126–27.
4. William C. Seitz, ed., *The Responsive Eye* (New York: Museum of Modern Art, 1965), 3. Anuszkiewicz studied with Albers at Yale from 1953 to 1955; Stanczak was a student of Albers between 1954 and 1956. Stanczak's 1964 show "Optical Paintings" at the Martha Jackson Gallery served as the origin of the term "op art."
5. Josef Albers, "Op Art and/or Perceptual Effects," *Yale Scientific Magazine* 11:2 (November 1965), 9 (Albers's emphasis). For an explanation of Albers's concern with the term "op art," see Josef Albers, *Search Versus Re-Search* (Hartford, CT: Trinity College Press, 1969), 20–21.
6. Barrett, *Op Art*, 112.

7. In Brian de Palma's 1965 documentary *The Responsive Eye*, produced by the Museum of Modern Art in conjunction with the "The Responsive Eye" exhibition, Albers remarks, "I had to wait fifty years until people finally looked to me as if they look with my eyes. Finally, this is acceptable. That took fifty years…."

8. Both Seitz and Greenberg included works by Walter Darby Bannard, Gene Davis, Thomas Downing, Paul Feeley, Ellsworth Kelly, Alexander Liberman, Morris Louis, Kenneth Noland, Ludwig Sander, and Frank Stella in their exhibitions. Seitz and Alloway included works by Feeley, Kelly, Downing, Noland, Stella, Agnes Martin, Larry Poons, and Leon Smith in their exhibitions.

9. See Seitz, *The Responsive Eye*, 5–9. He also wrote an essay for *Vogue* in which he condemned the mass media for their promotion of Op Art and the "oversimplification of art publicity." See William C. Seitz, "The New Perceptual Art," *Vogue* (U.S.), February 15, 1965, 79–80, 142–43. Although the term "op art" is thought widely to have been coined by Jon Borgzinner in an unattributed piece for *Time* in October 1964, Joe Houston has noted that Donald Judd first used the term in a review of Julian Stanczak's work in the October 1964 issue of *Arts Magazine*. See Joe Houston, *Optic Nerve: Perceptual Art of the 1960s* (London: Merrell Pub. Ltd., 2007), 57–58.

10. See Clement Greenberg, ed., *Post Painterly Abstraction* (Los Angeles: Los Angeles County Museum of Art, 1964), n.p.

11. See Clement Greenberg, "Modernist Painting," *Arts Yearbook* 4 (1961): 103–8; reprinted in John O'Brian, ed., *Clement Greenberg: The Collected Essays and Criticism, IV: Modernism with a Vengeance, 1957–1969* (Chicago: University of Chicago Press, 1993).

12. For a comprehensive assessment of the significance of opticality to Greenberg, see Caroline A. Jones, *Eyesight Alone: Clement Greenberg's Modernism and the Bureaucratization of the Senses* (Chicago: University of Chicago Press, 2005).

13. Lawrence Alloway, ed., *Systemic Painting* (New York: Solomon R. Guggenheim Museum, 1966), 11–21.

14. Greenberg, *Post Painterly Abstraction*, n.p.

15. I have written elsewhere about the ways in which Albers's practice was not in keeping with Greenberg's aesthetics. See "Pedagogic Objects: Josef Albers, Greenbergian Modernism and the Bauhaus in America," in Jeffrey Saletnik and Robin Schuldenfrei, eds., *Bauhaus Construct: Fashioning Identity, Discourse and Modernism* (New York: Routledge, 2009), 83–102. Rosalind Krauss's writing on the tactile aspects of perceptual art also is significant to this end. See Rosalind Krauss, "Afterthoughts on 'Op,'" *Art International* 9:5 (June 1965): 75–76.

16. Alloway, *Systemic Painting*, 19.

17. Josef Albers, *Formulation : Articulation* (New York: H. N. Abrams, 1972), n.p.

18. Donald Judd, "In the Galleries," *Arts Magazine* 39:2 (November 1964); repr. in *Donald Judd: Complete Writings, 1959–1975* (Halifax, N.S.: Press of the Nova Scotia College of Art and Design, 1975): 141–44.

19. Barbara Rose, "Beyond Vertigo: Optical Art at the Modern," *Artforum* 7 (April 1965), 32.

20. Barbara Rose, "Beyond Vertigo," 30, 31, 33 (my emphasis). For an assessment of the critical response to op art, see Pamela M. Lee, "Bridget Riley's Eye/Body Problem," *October* 98 (October 2001): 27–46.

21. "Notes on Op Art" in Lawrence Alloway, *Topics in American Art Since 1945* (New York: Norton, 1975), 239–44.
22. "Fashions in Living: Op-art-ment," *Vogue* (U.S.) February 1970, 122–25; *Vogue* (U.S.), June 1965, 3. The image credit for the cover of the 1970 magazine announced the imminent release of Fabergé Cosmetics' new "Make-OP."
23. See Milton H. Greene, "It's OP from Toe to Top," *Life*, April 16, 1965, 52–54.
24. Josef Albers, "Op Art and/or Perceptual Effects," 9. See also Rudolf Arnheim, *Art and Visual Perception: A Psychology of the Creative Eye* (Berkeley: University of California Press, 1954).
25. Josef Albers, *Interaction of Color* (New Haven: Yale University Press, 1963).
26. Albers listed the colors used on the verso of the work as, from center: "Cadmium Yellow Light (Grumbacher I.) / Naples Yellow Deep (Rhenish) / Naples Yellow (Utrecht) / Pure Cadmium Yellow Deep (Rhenish) / all in one primary coat." See object file for 29:1997, Saint Louis Art Museum.
27. Rosalind Krauss, "Afterthoughts on 'Op,'" *Art International* 9:5 (June 1965), 75–76.
28. Irwin's painting *Untitled* (1963) was included in the exhibition. Larry Bell also was included in the show, exhibiting *Glass Sculpture Number 10* (1964).
29. Quoted in Lawrence Weschler, *Seeing Is Forgetting the Name of the Thing One Sees* (Berkeley: University of California Press, 1982), 152. For a detailed description of the installation, see chapter 13, "The Room at the Museum of Modern Art," 147–54.
30. See Robert Irwin, *Being and Circumstance: Notes Toward a Conditional Art* (Larkspur Landing, Calif.: Lapis Press, 1985).
31. Quoted in Carol Diehl, "Robert Irwin's Doors of Perception," *Art in America* 87:12 (December 1999): 76–83.

Cat. 32: Josef Albers, Color study, n.d. Oil on blotting paper, 3 1/8 x 11 15/16 in. (7.9 x 30.3 cm). The Josef and Anni Albers Foundation (1976.2.1374).

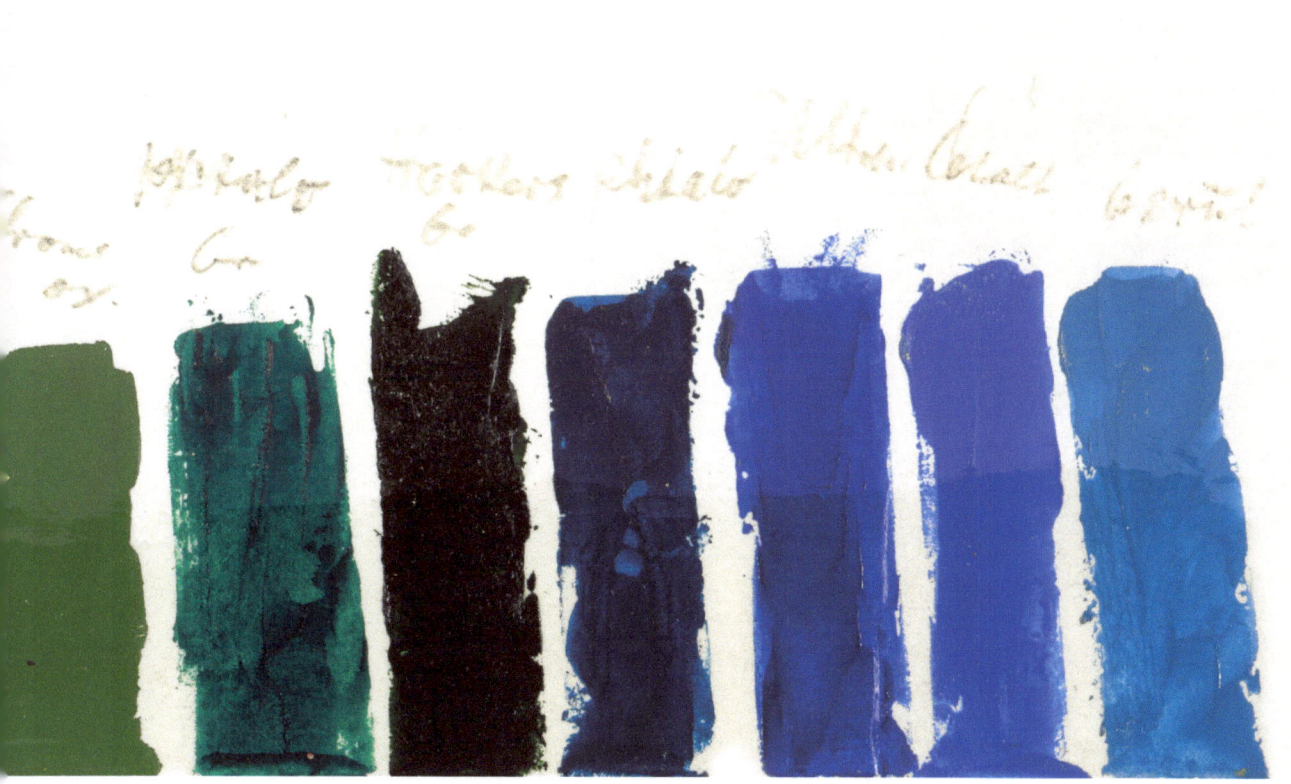

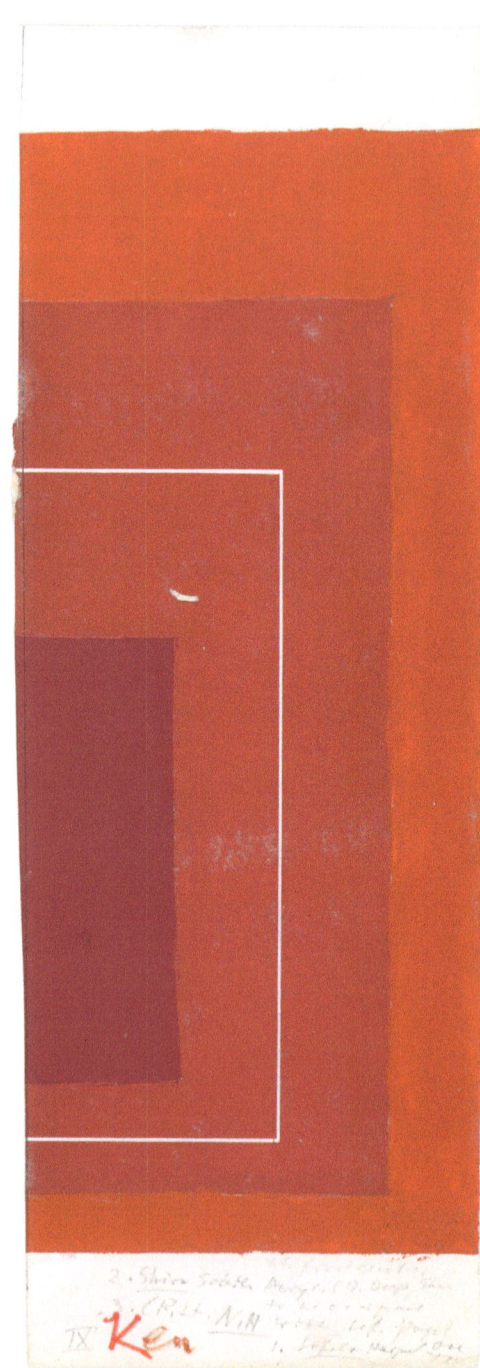

Cat. 33: Josef Albers, Color study (*Homage to the Square/White Line Square*), n.d. Oil on blotting paper, 13 1/8 x 4 13/16 in. (33.3 x 12.2 cm). The Josef and Anni Albers Foundation (1976.2.1394).

Josef Albers and the Science of Seeing

Susan R. Barry

In 1972, when Josef Albers was in his eighties, he published *Formulation : Articulation*, a set of two boxed portfolios of silkscreen prints. With these pieces, Albers continued his lifelong exploration of the basic elements that make up an image—line, contour, lightness, and color. He aimed for simplicity, discipline, and efficiency, and wrote,

> In my own work
> I am content to compete
> with myself
> and to search with simple palette
> and with simple color for manifold instrumentation.[1]

At the time Josef Albers composed *Formulation : Articulation*, scientists were using microelectrodes to eavesdrop on the behavior of individual neurons in the visual brain.[2] In a striking confluence of science and art, they discovered that neurons early on in the visual pathway attend specifically to the very same elements—line, contour, lightness, and color—that had preoccupied Albers for more than forty years.

Lines and Contours

Consider, for example, Albers's lyrical abstract work *In the Water* (fig. 28). Although *In the Water* contains only straight lines, the viewer perceives many curvy lines sculpting vase-like figures running from top to bottom. In an analogous way, we see lines in nature where there are none, a phenomenon that is reflected in even the simplest drawing. While an artist may draw an oval to represent a person's face, no such outline exists in real life. Is there something about our visual wiring that causes us to seek out such lines?

Light from the sun or reflected off objects is absorbed by the rod and cone cells in the retina at the back of the eye. Although rods and cones absorb the light

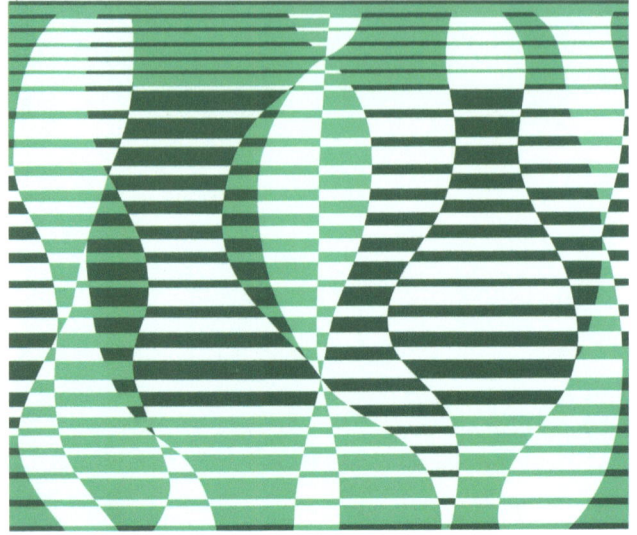 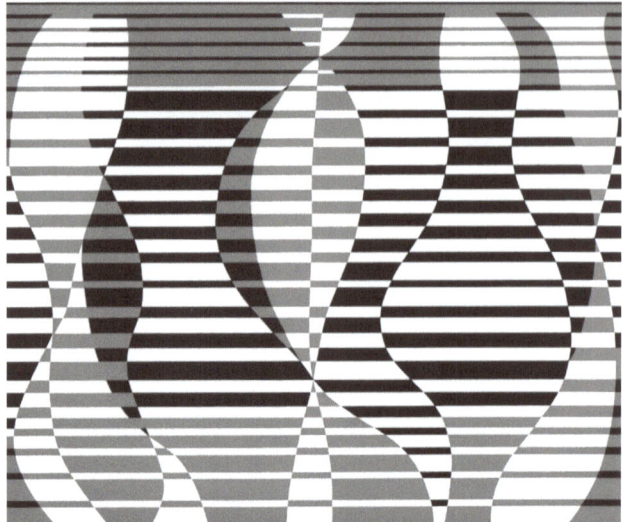

Figure 28 (left): Josef Albers, *Formulation : Articulation*, Folio I / Folder 2 ["In the Water"], 1972. Screenprint, 15 x 20 in. (38.1 x 50.8 cm), Mead Art Museum, Amherst College, gift of the Alan M. Sternlieb Study Collection (1979.103.1.2.a). Cat. 11.

Figure 29 (right): Author-created grayscale version of figure 28.

directly, we do not see with these cells. Before we have a conscious sensation of sight, information from rods and cones must make its way over several synaptic connections to the visual cortex located in the back of the brain and then to additional visual processing areas. With cats as their experimental animals, David Hubel and Torsten Wiesel made some of the first recordings of neurons in the primary visual cortex, the first area of the visual cortex to receive input from the eyes and a major gateway to higher visual areas. Initially, they attempted to stimulate these cells by projecting small spots of light, but with little success. After hours of recordings, they finally discovered that an individual cell responds not to spots, but to bars of light or dark in a particular small region of the visual field. Indeed, each neuron is sensitive to a narrow range of orientations, some preferring horizontal bars, others vertical bars, and still others bars at various oblique angles. For every point in our visual field there are cells that are sensitive to each orientation.[3] As light information is communicated from one cell to another along the visual pathway, we first detect a border or contour, then its orientation, and then the changes in orientation in order to perceive corners and curves.[4]

Although Albers had no knowledge of Hubel and Wiesel's study, he came to the same conclusion about the tendency of our visual system to seek out lines and contours. In his drawing classes he gave his students exercises in line control and measurement and taught them to represent objects "first and mainly by using lines, not shading."[5] Regarding *In the Water*, he wrote, "All lines exist only mathematically, that is, not by themselves but only as boundaries between different color areas."[6] Thus, when we gaze at the print and follow its sinuous curves, we are witnessing a particularly beautiful example of our own visual processes at work.

Lightness (Value)

The borders between the different horizontal lines in *In the Water* are defined by differences in both color and lightness. When the color is removed (fig. 29), the grayscale image allows us to see only the light and dark borders between the horizontal lines. However, we still see the curvy lines and figures.

Hence, in this image (though not in all cases), borders can be distinguished by lightness alone. Artists use the term "value" to define this sense of light and dark.[7]

Much more of our visual circuitry is devoted to signaling lightness than to signaling color, so we can easily distinguish levels of lightness in a picture made up of different shades of gray. However, most of us have a much harder time judging levels of lightness in a colored image. As Albers was well aware, sensitivity to lightness must be trained. In his now legendary art classes, he would confront his students with several pairs of colors, as in the figure below (fig. 30), and ask them to judge which color of the pair was darker and which was lighter.

According to his report, 60 percent of his students answered incorrectly![8] They would have had more success if they had looked at the same image in grayscale (fig. 31).[9] In each of the pairs, the upper member is easily seen as darker.

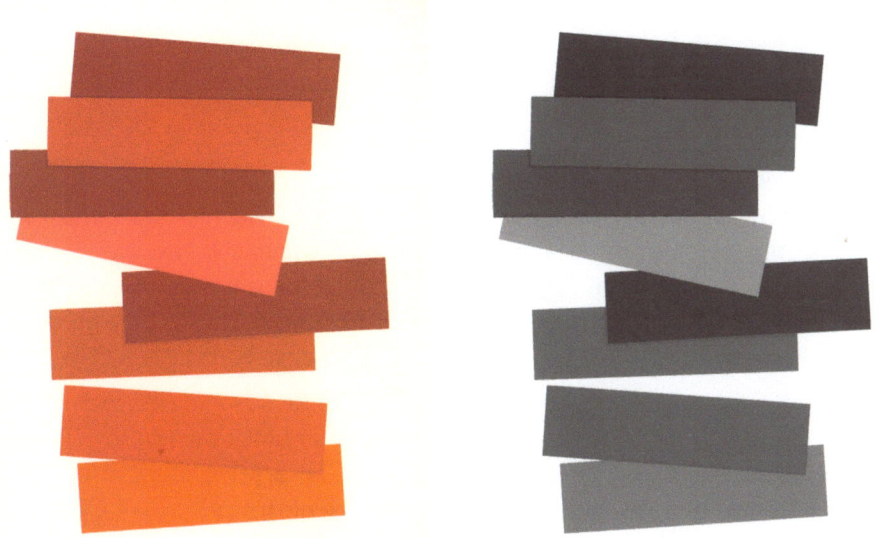

Figure 30 (left): Plate V-3 from Josef Albers, *Interaction of Color* (1963). Image courtesy the Josef and Anni Albers Foundation/Yale University Press.

Figure 31 (right): Author-created grayscale version of figure 30.

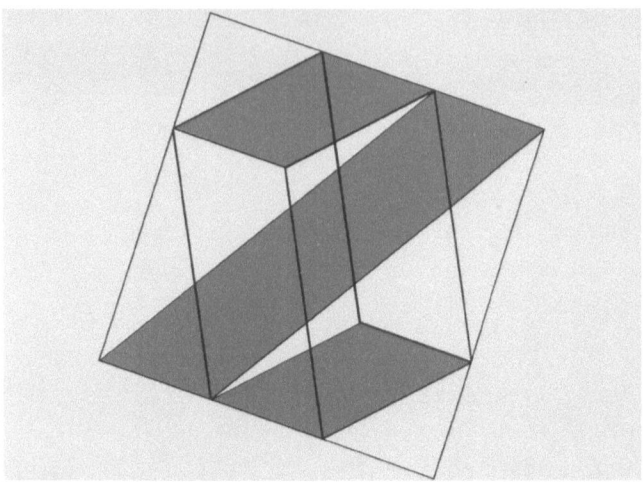 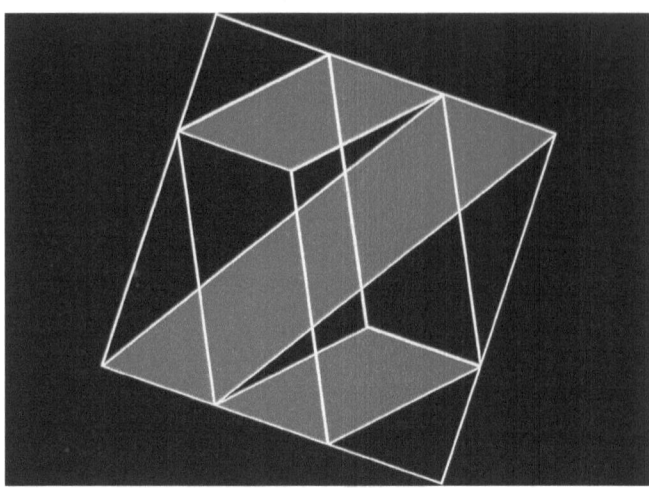

Figure 32a (left): Josef Albers, *Formulation : Articulation*, Folio II / Folder 16, 1972. Screenprint, 15 x 20 in. (38.1 x 50.8 cm). Mead Art Museum, Amherst College, gift of the Alan M. Sternlieb Study Collection (1979.103.2.16.a). Cat. 26.

Figure 32b (right): Josef Albers, *Formulation : Articulation*, Folio II / Folder 16, 1972. Screenprint, 15 x 20 in. (38.1 x 50.8 cm). Mead Art Museum, Amherst College, gift of the Alan M. Sternlieb Study Collection (1979.103.2.16.b). Cat. 27.

To train lightness perception, Albers had the students collect gray cutouts from magazines and then arrange the images from darkest to lightest. As these arrangements were made, his students not only learned to discriminate different degrees of lightness, but also achieved other insights. In the gray compositions by Albers above, for example (figs. 32a and 32b), the two Zs are made up of the same middle gray value.

We see them as very different, however, because the *Z* on the left is darker than its background, causing it to appear even darker, while the *Z* on the right is lighter than its background, causing it to appear lighter. This example illustrates what Albers called the "discrepancy between physical fact and psychic effect."[10]

Color

Albers called color the "most relative medium in art," and our perception of color is a similarly complicated phenomenon.[11] Part of the reason for this complexity is that, technically speaking, there is no color in the physical universe. What we perceive as color is really light of different wavelengths and intensities. Therefore, the perception of color, just like the sensation of pain or the feeling of pleasure, requires an individual to experience it.

The color spectrum, starting with the shortest light wavelengths that we can see and moving to the longest, ranges from violet to blue to green to yellow to orange to red. Color perception begins with the absorption of light by short wavelength, medium wavelength, and long wavelength cone cells.[12] Each type of cone cell responds to a broad range of wavelengths but has a particular

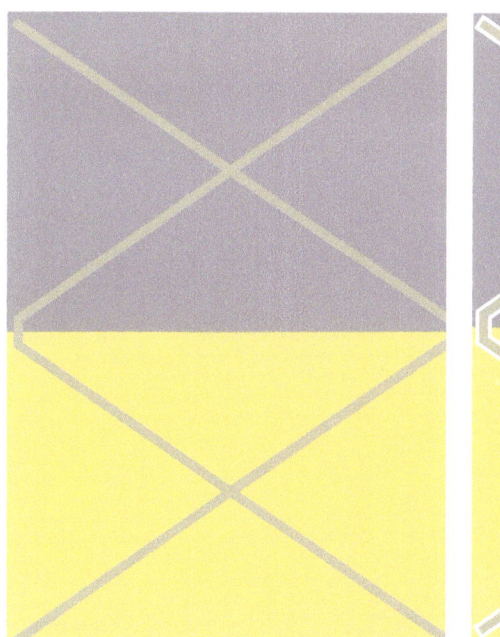 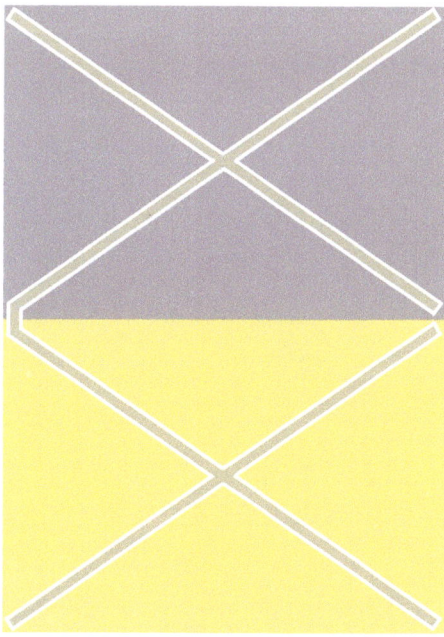

Figure 33 (left): Plate VI-3 from Josef Albers, *Interaction of Color* (1963). Image courtesy the Josef and Anni Albers Foundation/Yale University Press.

Figure 34 (right): Author's alteration of Plate VI-3 from Josef Albers, *Interaction of Color* (1963). Image courtesy the Josef and Anni Albers Foundation/Yale University Press. Adapted from figure 3 in Bevil Conway, "Color Consilience: Color through the Lens of Art Practice, History, Philosophy, and Neuroscience," *Annals of the New York Academy of Sciences* 1251 (2012): 77–94.

peak sensitivity. The peak sensitivity is in the violets for the short wavelength cones, the greens for the medium wavelength cones, and the yellows for the long wavelength cones. Thus a given wavelength of light excites the three types of cone cells to different extents, and the relative strength of their responses contributes to the color we see. A color that we perceive as green excites the short wavelength cone cells to a small extent, the long wavelength cone cells to a greater extent, and the medium wavelength cone cells the most.

However, the perception of color, like the perception of light and dark, is based also on the context in which a particular color is perceived. Just as the lightness of the gray Zs in figures 5a and 5b appears to vary depending on the background, a color's appearance depends upon the colors that surround it. For example, as Bevil Conway discussed in a recent paper, the two Xs in the figure created by Albers above (fig. 33) are actually the same color, or hue; both reflect the same light wavelengths back to our eyes.[13] (This can be seen particularly clearly at the point on the middle left where the two Xs connect.) Yet the X on the gray background looks yellow, while the X on the yellow background looks gray. As with the Zs, the visual system in each case compares and subtracts the background color from the central image.

This influence operates the most strongly when the two colors are directly adjacent to each other. As Conway illustrated, the influence is mitigated simply

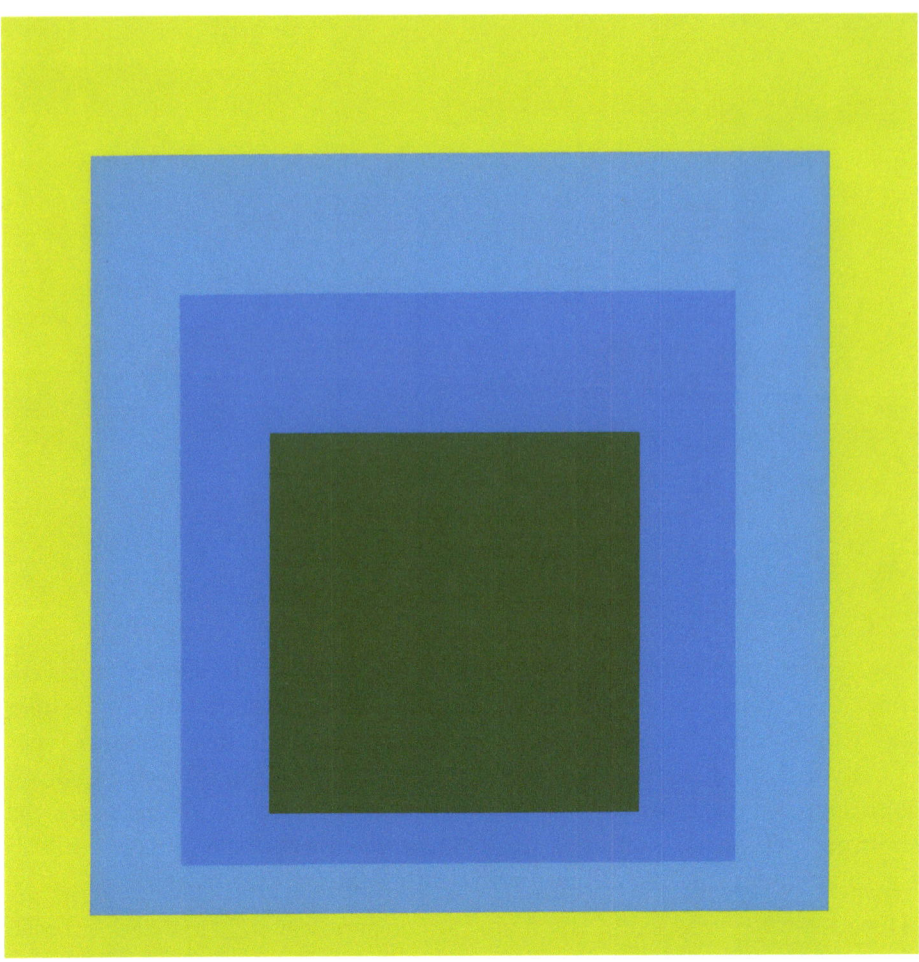

Figure 35a: Josef Albers, *Formulation : Articulation*, Folio I / Folder 5 [*Homage to the Square*], 1972. Screenprint, 15 x 20 in. (38.1 x 50.8 cm), Mead Art Museum, Amherst College, gift of the Alan M. Sternlieb Study Collection (1979.103.1.5.a). Cat. 12.

by placing a white border around the Xs (fig. 34), which greatly reduces the apparent color difference.

Intriguingly, scientists have uncovered neurons in the primary visual cortex that fire most actively not in response to a single color, but to the juxtaposition of two colors, particularly red next to cyan (a greenish blue), yellow next to blue, and black next to white.[14] Although these neurophysiological discoveries were made after Albers taught and painted, he was well aware of these interactions of color. In his color classes, for example, he would distribute papers of different colors and instruct his students to place a small patch of one color against a background of another. With the right choice of two different background colors, the identical central color could appear as two very different hues. Conversely, two different colors against different backgrounds could be made to look like one.[15] He wrote, "Color, in my opinion, behaves like man—in

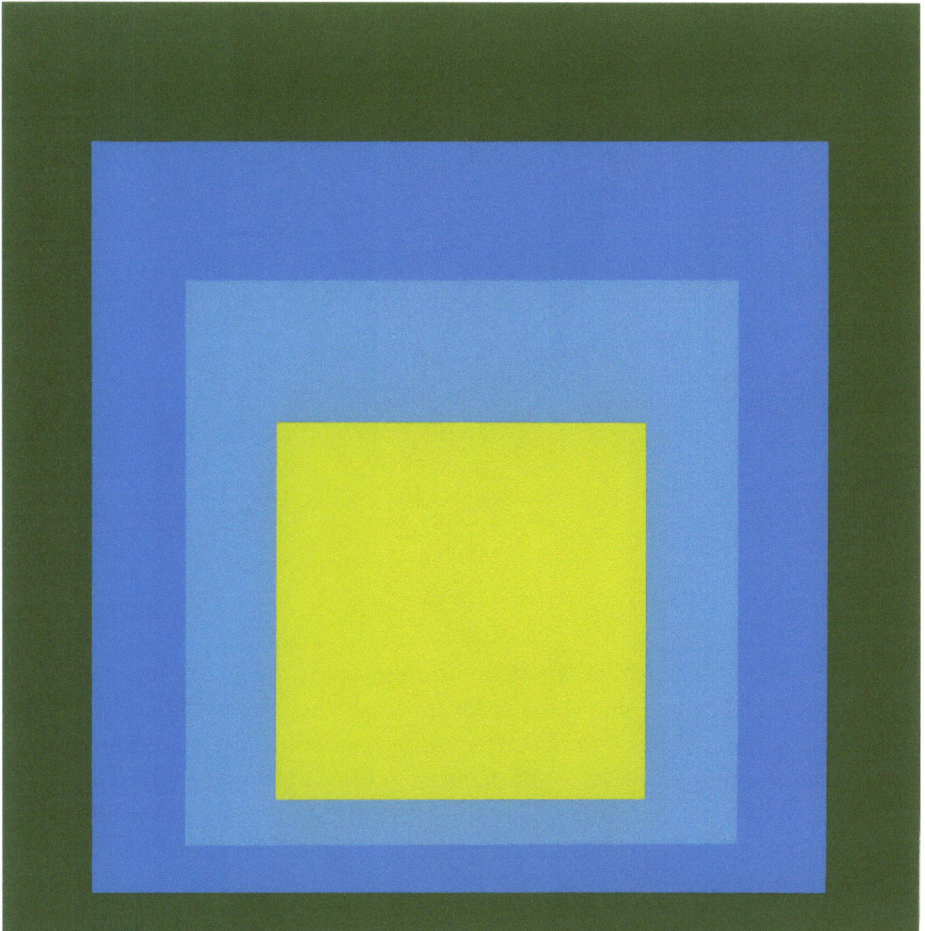

Figure 35b: Josef Albers, *Formulation : Articulation*, Folio I / Folder 5 [*Homage to the Square*], 1972. Screenprint, 15 x 20 in. (38.1 x 50.8 cm), Mead Art Museum, Amherst College, gift of the Alan M. Sternlieb Study Collection (1979.103.1.5.b). Cat. 13.

two distinct ways: first in self-realization and then in the realizations of relationships with others...."[16]

In his remarkable series *Homage to the Square*, Albers, using a palette knife and paint directly from the tube, placed one square immediately adjacent to the next with no gaps in between (figs. 35a and 35b) so that one color had its strongest effect upon its neighbor.[17] In the two versions of *Homage to the Square* shown above, the same four colors are used in the same proportions, but the arrangement of the colors is reversed, changing the appearance and weight of the colors in the two images. The two prints also produce different effects on different viewers. In one version, the color of the central square may appear to come forward for some people but not for others. Even the way the pictures are scanned may differ from one individual to the next. While a casual observer might notice

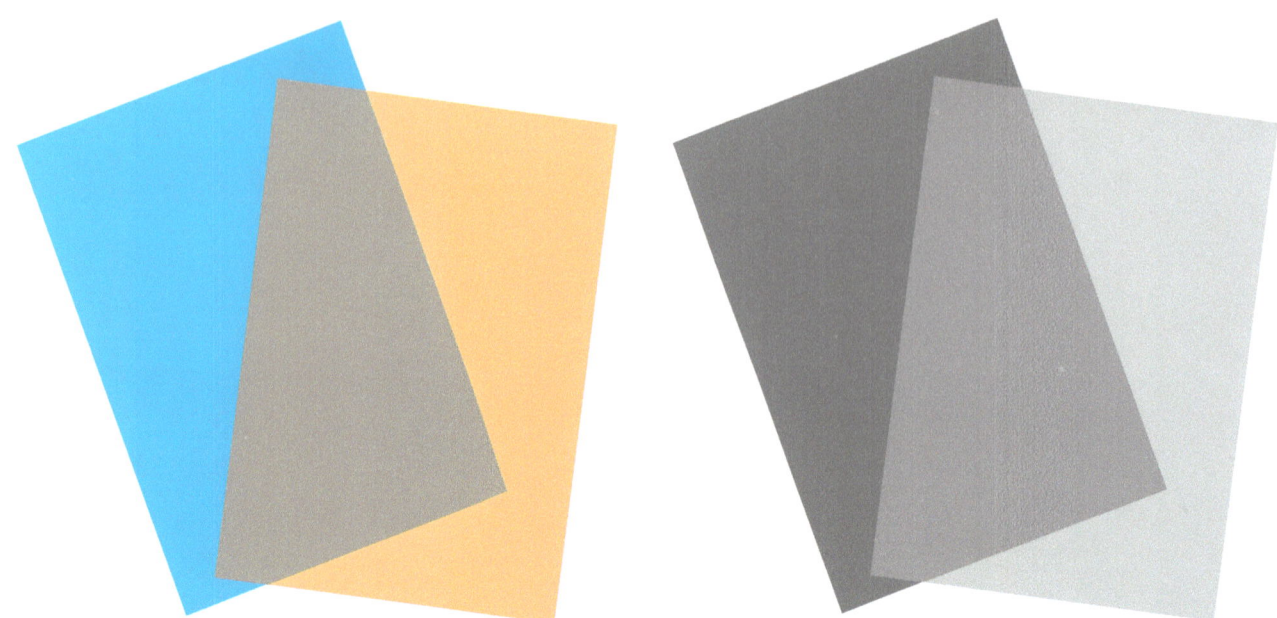

Figure 36 (left): Transparency color exercise made with the App version of Josef Albers, *Interaction of Color* (2013). Image courtesy the Josef and Anni Albers Foundation/Yale University Press.

Figure 37 (right): Author-created grayscale version of figure 36.

the outer color first, a painter, for example, might read the print from the central square outward because that is the order in which an artist would paint it. (This procedure is mostly a practical matter; Albers recounts the story of how his father taught him to paint a door by starting in the middle and painting outward so that he didn't get the cuffs of his shirt dirty!).[18] Still other observers might attend first to their favorite color or be drawn most to the grouping of colors, such as the two blues.

The response of the visual system to adjacent colors illustrates a general property of perception. Under many circumstances, our brain does not care about absolutes, such as the exact wavelength of a given light ray. What it cares about is contrast, particularly contrast across local boundaries. By highlighting what is different between one area and another, like the *X*s against the differently colored backgrounds, we are better able to pick out an object from its surroundings, to distinguish figure from ground.

For Albers, the importance of the relationship between colors, as opposed to the color itself, took on a moral character. When Albers wrote that colors exist in terms of "relationships with others" he was not only making a statement about perception or aesthetics. He thought of color, he said, as both "an individual" and "a member of society"; "I've handled color as man should behave.... And from all this, you may conclude that I consider ethics and aesthetics as one."[19]

Seeing the Whole Picture

However, vision depends upon far more than the piecemeal construction of a scene from the basic elements of line, lightness, and color. This, too, was a concept that Albers demonstrated in his artwork and classes.[20] Albers was intrigued, for example, by the phenomenon of transparency. In one exercise, he would challenge his students to take a piece of paper that was opaque, and by placing it next to other colored papers, make it appear transparent or translucent.[21] One example is shown in figure 36.

In this figure, a piece of opaque brown paper has been placed between the blue and orange ones. This juxtaposition makes the brown paper appear translucent, as if it is the part of the orange paper that is overlapping with and partially blocking our view of the blue paper below it. A grayscale version of this image (fig. 37) shows that the lightness or value of the brown paper is at an intermediate level between that of the other two. This lightness arrangement follows a general rule for transparency: the transparent region must be of intermediate lightness with the regions that it borders.[22] If the brown paper had been darker or lighter than both of its neighbors, the illusion of transparency would disappear.

In addition, the illusion of transparency is maintained only if we look at the picture as a whole. If the view of either the orange or blue paper is obscured so that the brown paper is viewed next to only one of its neighbors, it appears opaque. Thus a scene cannot be perceived correctly in terms of a piecemeal examination of its individual parts but must be viewed as an integrated whole.

Albers delighted particularly in the creation of ambiguous figures or images that can be interpreted in more than one way. One example is the work titled *Steps*, the first work in his *Formulation : Articulation* portfolio (fig. 38). The larger image on the right appears to be a set of steps. Since the lowest step is the widest, we see it first and read the steps as moving upward and away from us. But the smaller figure on the left is ambiguous. It can be seen as a set of steps moving toward us or away from us, a set in which only the middle step is receding, or in five other ways.

Art, Albers felt, much more than nature, could provide such challenges to our visual perception. Although all visual stimuli are potentially ambiguous, we are usually able to exploit a great number of clues in order to make sense of the real

Figure 38: Josef Albers, *Formulation : Articulation*, Folio I / Folder I ["Steps"], 1972. Screenprint, 15 x 20 in. (38.1 x 50.8 cm. Mead Art Museum, Amherst College; gift of the Alan M. Sternlieb Study Collection (1979.103.1.1.a).

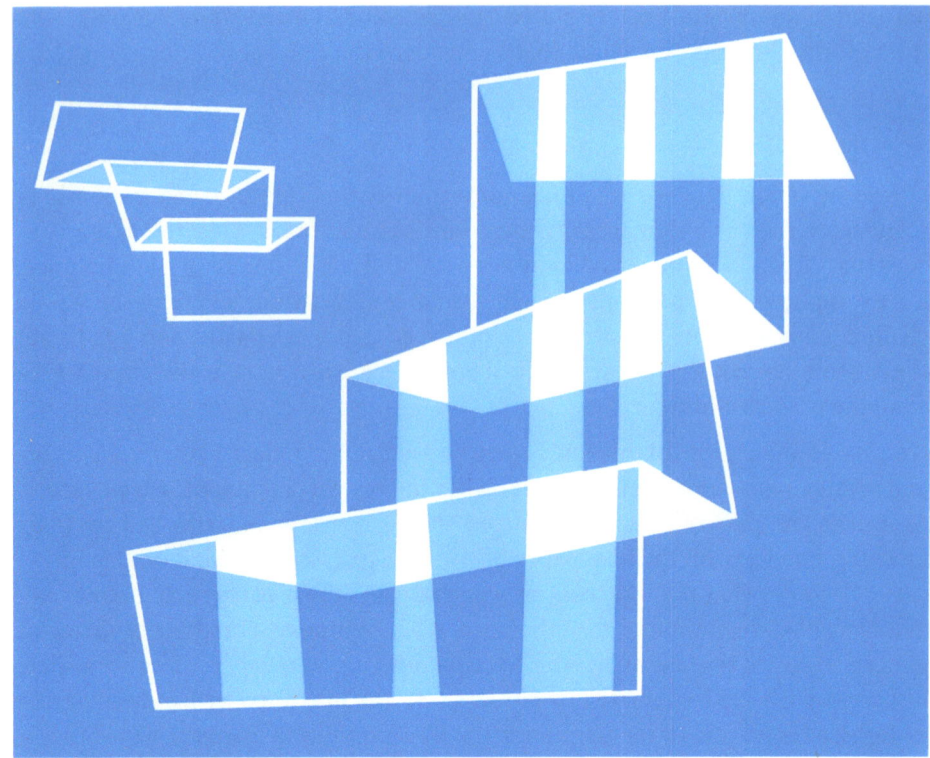

objects around us. While looking at an actual staircase, for example, we exploit information from shadows, size, perspective, stereo vision, and its changing appearance as we move. By removing such clues in the small figure in *Steps*, Albers forces us to pay attention to the basic elements of the drawing—the lines and their interactions.

Formulation : Articulation includes many additional images from his *Graphic Tectonic* series that can be interpreted in multiple ways. Two examples are *Synopsis* (fig. 39a) and *Syntax* (fig. 39b). About the latter painting Albers wrote, "Thus we cannot remain in a single viewpoint; we need more for the sake of FREE VISION."[23] Indeed, in his classes, Albers emphasized the role of changing viewpoints on perception by having his students view a target as they moved around it. Even when we look steadily at an image, our eyes make tiny scanning movements, and these shifts may contribute to multiple readings of an ambiguous figure. For example, the familiar Necker cube (fig. 40) can be seen in two ways, with either the cube's lower surface or right surface facing front.

These two views are associated with slightly different eye positions.[24] Thus "free vision" in the most literal sense—free movement of the eyes—allows us to

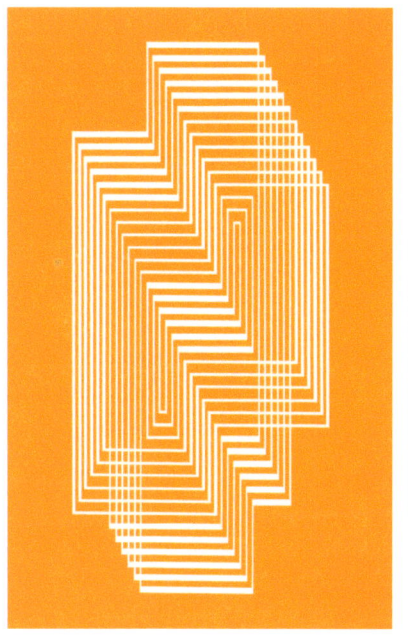
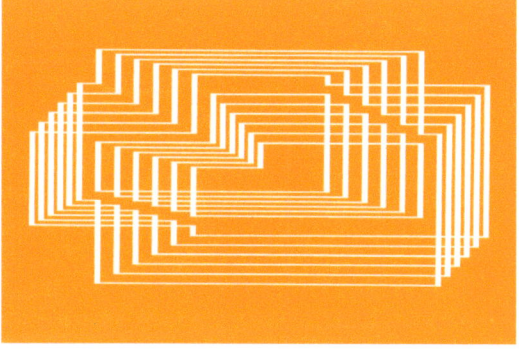

Figure 39a (left): Josef Albers, *Formulation : Articulation*, Folio I / Folder 31 ["Synopsis"], 1972. Screenprint, 15 x 20 in. (38.1 x 50.8 cm). Mead Art Museum, Amherst College, gift of the Alan M. Sternlieb Study Collection (1979.103.1.31.a). Cat. 23.

Figure 39b (right): Josef Albers, *Formulation Articulation*, Folio I / Folder 31 ["Syntax"], 1972. Screenprint, 15 x 20 in. (38.1 x 50.8 cm). Mead Art Museum, Amherst College, gift of the Alan M. Sternlieb Study Collection (1979.103.1.31.b). Cat. 24.

engage with ambiguous figures, from the iconic Necker cube to Albers's more complex creations, and to switch from one interpretation to another.

Exactly how we make the perceptual switch between alternative readings of *Steps, Syntax*, or any other ambiguous figure is not known, but science offers some intriguing clues. While we may shift from one interpretation to another, we never entertain more than one at a time. The best we can do is switch rapidly back and forth.

Brain imaging reveals that far more of the brain is involved in viewing an ambiguous figure than in viewing a stable, unambiguous one. Both types of images will excite the entire visual system, but the ambiguous figure, such as the smaller image in *Steps*, will cause greater activation of areas toward the front of the brain, including regions of the fronto-parietal and frontal cortices.[25] Taking into account factors such as experience, expectations, and even our mood, these brain areas then provide higher-level

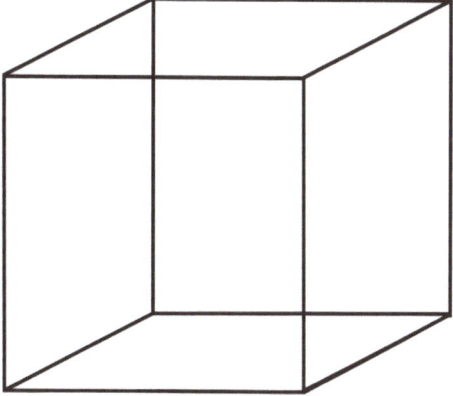

Figure 40: Example of the iconic Necker cube.

Josef Albers and the Science of Seeing

hypotheses about what we are viewing, entering into a dialogue with the visual areas of the brain to confirm or reject these hypotheses. For an image that can be interpreted in many different ways, this dialogue will be sustained for the entire time we view the image. Thus Albers's *Formulation : Articulation* portfolio, like his *Graphic Tectonic* series as a whole and indeed, like all his art and teaching, achieves "manifold instrumentation" with only a "simple palette," enlightening us all about visual perception and providing rich stimulation for the brain.

Notes

1. Josef Albers, *Formulation : Articulation* (London: Thames and Hudson, 2006), artist's notes corresponding to folder II:18.
2. David H. Hubel and Torsten N. Wiesel, "Receptive Fields of Single Neurons in the Cat's Striate Cortex," *Journal of Physiology* 148 (1959): 574–91; David H. Hubel and Torsten N. Wiesel, "Receptive Fields, Binocular Interaction and Functional Architecture in the Cat's Visual Cortex, *Journal of Physiology* 160 (1962): 106–54; David H. Hubel, *Eye, Brain, and Vision* (New York: Scientific American Library, 1995); Margaret Livingstone, *Vision and Art: The Biology of Seeing*, revised and expanded edition (New York: Abrams, 2014).
3. Hubel and Wiesel, "Receptive Fields of Single Neurons"; Hubel and Wiesel, "Receptive Fields, Binocular Interaction and Functional Architecture"; Hubel, *Eye, Brain, and Vision*.
4. Hubel, *Eye, Brain, and Vision*; Livingstone, *Vision and Art*.
5. Frederick A. Horowitz and Brenda Danilowitz, *Josef Albers: To Open Eyes* (London: Phaidon Press, 2009), 153.
6. Albers, *Formulation : Articulation*, artist's notes corresponding to folder I:2.
7. Livingstone, *Vision and Art*.
8. Josef Albers, *Interaction of Color*, revised and expanded edition (New Haven: Yale University Press, 2006).
9. A grayscale image should provide the gray or lightness level of each region or pixel of the figure. There is no universally accepted way to convert an image to grayscale, so each computer program may do the conversion slightly differently while also incorporating other information from the picture.
10. Albers, *Interaction of Color*, 8.
11. Albers, *Interaction of Color*, 1.
12. Livingstone, *Vision and Art*.
13. Bevil Conway, "Color Consilience: Color through the Lens of Art Practice, History, Philosophy, and Neuroscience," *Annals of the New York Academy of Sciences* 1251 (2012): 77–94. See also Bevil Conway, "Color Vision, Cones, and Color–Coding in the Cortex," *The Neuroscientist* 15 (2009): 274–90.
14. Conway, "Color Consilience."
15. Albers, *Interaction of Color*.
16. Albers, *Formulation : Articulation*, notes to folder II:17.

17. Nicholas Fox Weber, "The Artist as Alchemist," in *Josef Albers: A Retrospective* (New York: Simon R. Guggenheim Museum, 1988).
18. Weber, "The Artist as Alchemist."
19. Albers, *Formulation : Articulation*, notes to folder II:17.
20. Horowitz and Danilowitz, *Josef Albers*.
21. Albers, *Interaction of Color*.
22. Fabio Metelli, "The Perception of Transparency," *Scientific American* 230 (1974), 90–98; Barton L. Anderson and Jonathan Winawer, "Image Segmentation and Lightness Perception," *Nature* 434 (2005): 79–83.
23. Albers, *Formulation : Articulation*, notes to folder I:31.
24. Wolfgang Einhauser, Kevan A. C. Martin, and Peter König, "Are Switches in Perception of the Necker Cube Related to Eye Position?" *European Journal of Neuroscience* 20 (2004): 2811–18.
25. Megan Wang, Daniel Arteaga, and Biyu J. He, "Brain Mechanisms for Simple Perception and Bistable Perception," *Proceedings of the National Academy of Sciences* 110 (2013): E3350–E3359, doi:10.1073/pnas.1221945110.

Cat. 34: Josef Albers, Color study, n.d. Oil on blotting paper, 3 1/8 x 12 in. (7.9 x 30.6 cm). The Josef and Anni Albers Foundation (1976.2.1471).

Contributors

Vanja Malloy is the curator of American art at the Mead Art Museum at Amherst College and the organizing editor and curator of *Intersecting Colors*. She has a longstanding research interest in the intersections of art and science and earned her Ph.D. at the Courtauld Institute of Art for her dissertation, "Rethinking Alexander Calder: Astronomy, Relativity, and Psychology."

Brenda Danilowitz is chief curator at the Josef and Anni Albers Foundation. She obtained her M.A. in art history from the University of the Witwatersrand, South Africa, where she taught from 1979 to 1986. She has organized several exhibitions and published articles and essays on contemporary South African art and on Josef and Anni Albers.

Sarah Lowengard is a member of the Faculty of Humanities and Social Sciences at Cooper Union in New York City. She is an artisan colormaker and art conservator as well as a historian of technology and science and conducts research on the subjects of color, color standards, and historical color production.

Karen Koehler is the Levin Professor of Art and Architectural History at Hampshire College, where she is also the director of the Institute for Curatorial Practice and a member of the Five College Architectural Studies Council. She has published widely on dialogues among art, architecture, and pictures, with a specialization in the Bauhaus, and has lectured widely on these subjects. She is currently writing on the double portrait in Bauhaus photography and completing an intellectual history of the architect Walter Gropius from the 1930s to the 1960s.

Jeffrey Saletnik teaches in the Department of Art History at Indiana University, Bloomington. He has published essays on Josef Albers, László Moholy-Nagy, and John Cage, and co-edited *Bauhaus Construct: Fashioning Identity, Discourse, and Modernism* (Routledge, 2010).

Susan R. Barry received her Ph.D. in biology from Princeton University in 1981 and is a professor of biological sciences and of neuroscience and behavior at Mount Holyoke College. She teaches a course on art, music, and the brain and is the author of *Fixing My Gaze: A Scientist's Journey into Seeing in Three Dimensions* (Basic Books, 2009).

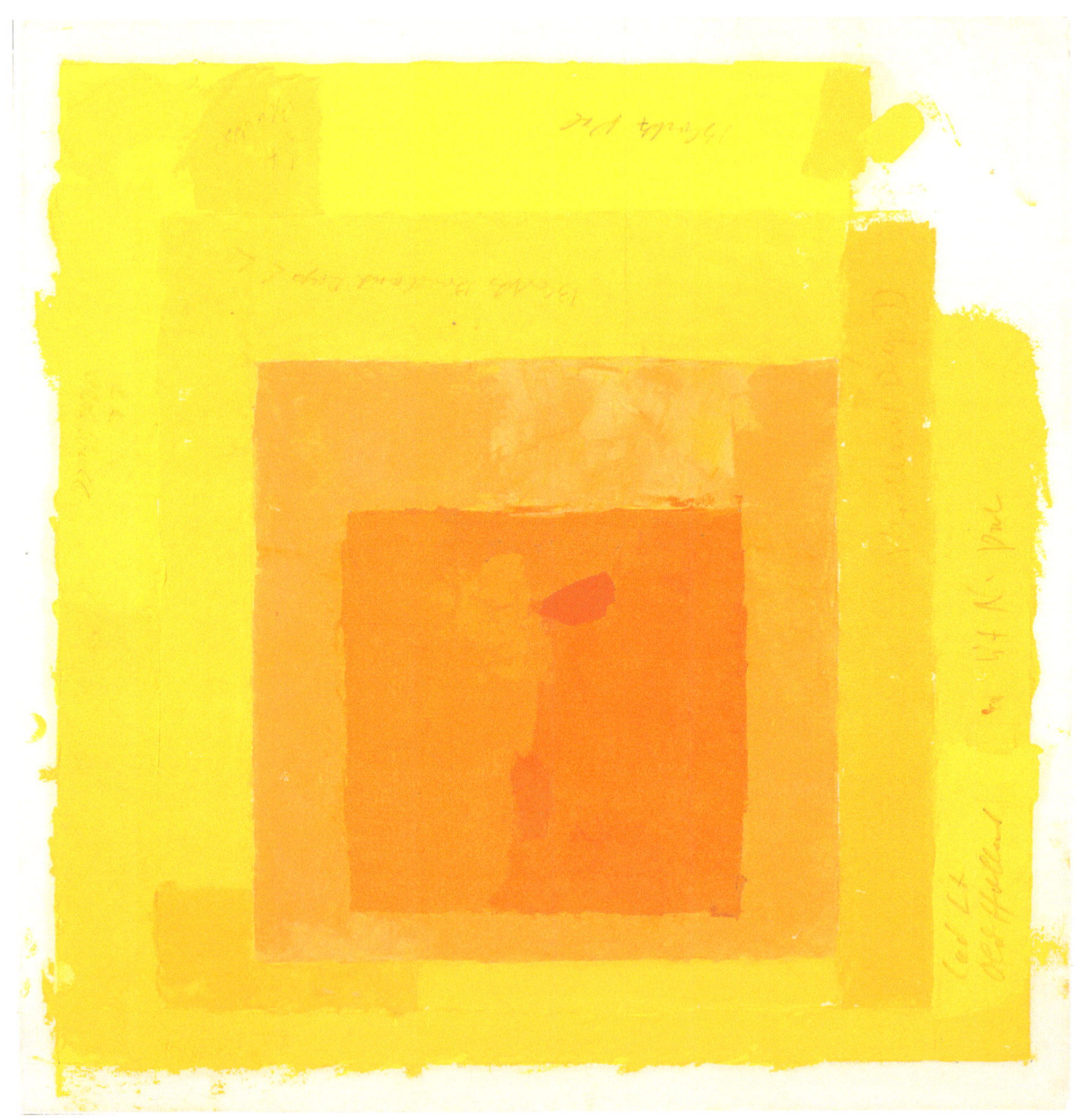

Cat. 38: Josef Albers, Color study for *Homage to the Square*, n.d. Oil and graphite on blotting paper, 12 x 12 in. (30.5 x 30.5 cm). The Josef and Anni Albers Foundation (1976.2.79).

Exhibition Checklist

1. Josef Albers
   American (born Germany), 1888–1976
   Stufen (Steps), 1931
   Sandblasted opaque flashed glass
   16 x 21 in. (40.6 x 53.3 cm)
   The Josef and Anni Albers Foundation,
   Bethany, Connecticut (2007.6.1)

2. Josef Albers
   American (born Germany), 1888–1976
   Heraldic, 1935
   Oil on stainless steel
   16 ¾ x 16 in. (42.5 x 40.6 cm)
   The Josef and Anni Albers Foundation,
   Bethany, Connecticut (1976.1.1863)

3. Josef Albers
   American (born Germany), 1888–1976
   Leaf Study II, ca. 1940
   Leaves on paper
   14 ½ x 18 3/8 in. (36.8 x 46.7 cm)
   The Josef and Anni Albers Foundation,
   Bethany, Connecticut (1976.9.2)

4. Josef Albers
   American (born Germany), 1888–1976
   Leaf Study I, ca. 1940
   Leaves on paper
   9 ½ x 18 in. (24.1 x 45.7 cm)
   The Josef and Anni Albers Foundation,
   Bethany, Connecticut (1976.9.9)

5. Josef Albers
   American (born Germany), 1888–1976
   Study for Homage to the Square: Rooted, 1961
   Oil on board
   30 x 30 in. (76.2 x 76.2 cm)
   Mead Art Museum, Amherst College
   Gift of Richard S. Zeisler, Class of 1937
   (1965.93)

6. Josef Albers
   American (born Germany), 1888–1976
   Interaction of Color, 1963
   First-edition book with silkscreen plates, letter-press, and offset lithography plates
   Published by Yale University Press,
   New Haven, 1963
   14 ½ x 11 x 5 ½ in. (36.8 x 27.9 x 13.9 cm)
   Robert Frost Library, Amherst College

7. Josef Albers
   American (born Germany), 1888–1976
   WLS XV, 1966
   Three-color aluminum plate lithograph
   20 ¾ x 20 ¾ in. (52.7 x 52.7 cm)
   The Josef and Albers Foundation,
   Bethany, Connecticut (1976.4.172.7)

8. Josef Albers
   American (born Germany), 1888–1976
   I-S Va 2, 1969
   Screenprint on Arches paper
   28 x 36 in. (71.1 x 91.4 cm)
   Mead Art Museum, Amherst College
   Gift of William W. Collins, Class of 1953, in
   Memory of Wortham Collins (1975.103)

9. Josef Albers
   American (born Germany), 1888–1976
   Study for print of *Steps*, ca. 1972
   Oil over offset printed image on paper
   7 5/8 x 9 5/8 in. (19.4 x 24.4 cm)
   The Josef and Anni Albers Foundation,
   Bethany, Connecticut (1976.2.205)

10. Josef Albers
    American (born Germany), 1888–1976
    Formulation : Articulation, Folio I / Folder I ["Steps"], 1972
    Screenprint
    15 x 20 in. (38.1 x 50.8 cm)
    Mead Art Museum, Amherst College
    Gift of the Alan M. Sternlieb Study Collection
    (1979.103.1.1.b)

11. Josef Albers
    American (born Germany), 1888–1976
    Formulation : Articulation, Folio I / Folder 2 ["In the Water"], 1972
    Screenprint
    15 x 20 in. (38.1 x 50.8 cm)
    Mead Art Museum, Amherst College
    Gift of the Alan M. Sternlieb Study Collection
    (1979.103.1.2.a)
    Fig. 28

12. Josef Albers
    American (born Germany), 1888–1976
    Formulation : Articulation, Folio I / Folder 5 ["Homage to the Square"], 1972
    Screenprint
    15 x 20 in. (38.1 x 50.8 cm)
    Mead Art Museum, Amherst College
    Gift of the Alan M. Sternlieb Study Collection
    (1979.103.1.5.a)
    Fig. 35a

13. Josef Albers
    American (born Germany), 1888–1976
    Formulation : Articulation, Folio I / Folder 5 ["Homage to the Square"], 1972
    Screenprint
    15 x 20 in. (38.1 x 50.8 cm)
    Mead Art Museum, Amherst College
    Gift of the Alan M. Sternlieb Study Collection
    (1979.103.1.5.b)
    Fig. 35b

14. Josef Albers
    American (born Germany), 1888–1976
    Formulation : Articulation, Folio I / Folder 6, 1972
    Screenprint
    15 x 20 in. (38.1 x 50.8 cm)
    Mead Art Museum, Amherst College
    Gift of the Alan M. Sternlieb Study Collection
    (1979.103.1.6.a)

15. Josef Albers
    American (born Germany), 1888–1976
    Formulation : Articulation, Folio I / Folder 15 ["Homage to the Square"], 1972
    Screenprint
    15 x 20 in. (38.1 x 50. 8 cm)
    Mead Art Museum, Amherst College
    Gift of the Alan M. Sternlieb Study Collection
    (1979.103.1.15.b)

16. Josef Albers
    American (born Germany), 1888–1976
    Formulation : Articulation, Folio I / Folder 16, 1972
    Screenprint
    15 x 20 in. (38.1 x 50.8 cm)
    Mead Art Museum, Amherst College
    Gift of the Alan M. Sternlieb Study Collection
    (1979.103.1.16.a)

17. Josef Albers
    American (born Germany), 1888–1976
    Formulation : Articulation, Folio I / Folder 17 ["Variants II"], 1972
    Screenprint
    15 x 20 in. (38.1 x 50.8 cm)
    Mead Art Museum, Amherst College
    Gift of the Alan M. Sternlieb Study Collection
    (1979.103.1.17.b)

18. Josef Albers
    American (born Germany), 1888–1976
    Formulation : Articulation, Folio I / Folder 18 ["Wrongly Rolled"], 1972
    Screenprint
    15 x 20 in. (38.1 x 50.8 cm)
    Mead Art Museum, Amherst College
    Gift of the Alan M. Sternlieb Study Collection
    (1979.103.1.18.b)

19. Josef Albers
    American (born Germany), 1888–1976
    Formulation : Articulation, Folio I / Folder 21 ["Skyscrapers"], 1972
    Screenprint
    15 x 20 in. (38.1 x 50.8 cm)
    Mead Art Museum, Amherst College
    Gift of the Alan M. Sternlieb Study Collection
    (1979.103.1.21.a)

20. Josef Albers
American (born Germany), 1888–1976
Formulation : Articulation, Folio I / Folder 29, 1972
Screenprint
15 x 20 in. (38.1 x 50.8 cm)
Mead Art Museum, Amherst College
Gift of the Alan M. Sternlieb Study Collection
(1979.103.1.29.a)

21. Josef Albers
American (born Germany), 1888–1976
Formulation : Articulation, Folio I / Folder 30 ["Variants II"], 1972
Screenprint
15 x 20 in. (38.1 x 50.8 cm)
Mead Art Museum, Amherst College
Gift of the Alan M. Sternlieb Study Collection
(1979.103.1.30.a)

22. Josef Albers
American (born Germany), 1888–1976
Formulation : Articulation, Folio I / Folder 30 ["Variants II"], 1972
Screenprint
15 x 20 in. (38.1 x 50.8 cm)
Mead Art Museum, Amherst College
Gift of the Alan M. Sternlieb Study Collection
(1979.103.1.30.b)

23. Josef Albers
American (born Germany), 1888–1976
Formulation : Articulation, Folio I / Folder 31 ["Synopsis"], 1972
Screenprint
15 x 20 in. (38.1 x 50.8 cm)
Mead Art Museum, Amherst College
Gift of the Alan M. Sternlieb Study Collection
(1979.103.1.31.a)
Fig. 39a

24. Josef Albers
American (born Germany), 1888–1976
Formulation : Articulation, Folio I / Folder 31 ["Syntax"], 1972
Screenprint
15 x 20 in. (38.1 x 50.8 cm)
Mead Art Museum, Amherst College
Gift of the Alan M. Sternlieb Study Collection
(1979.103.1.31.b)
Fig. 39b

25. Josef Albers
American (born Germany), 1888–1976
Formulation : Articulation, Folio II / Folder 15, 1972
Screenprint
15 x 20 in. (38.1 x 50.8 cm)
Mead Art Museum, Amherst College
Gift of the Alan M. Sternlieb Study Collection
(1979.103.2.15.a)

26. Josef Albers
American (born Germany), 1888–1976
Formulation : Articulation, Folio II / Folder 16, 1972
Screenprint
15 x 20 in. (38.1 x 50.8 cm)
Mead Art Museum, Amherst College
Gift of the Alan M. Sternlieb Study Collection
(1979.103.2.16.a)
Fig. 32a

27. Josef Albers
American (born Germany), 1888–1976
Formulation : Articulation, Folio II / Folder 16, 1972
Screenprint
15 x 20 in. (38.1 x 50.8 cm)
Mead Art Museum, Amherst College
Gift of the Alan M. Sternlieb Study Collection
(1979.103.2.16.b)
Fig. 32b

28. Josef Albers
American (born Germany), 1888–1976
Formulation : Articulation, Folio II / Folder 25, 1972
Screenprint
15 x 20 in. (38.1 x 50.8 cm)
Mead Art Museum, Amherst College
Gift of the Alan M. Sternlieb Study Collection
(1979.103.2.25.b)

29. Josef Albers
American (born Germany), 1888–1976
Formulation : Articulation, Folio II / Folder 32 ["Homage to the Square"], 1972
Screenprint
15 x 20 in. (38.1 x 50.8 cm)
Mead Art Museum, Amherst College
Gift of the Alan M. Sternlieb Study Collection
(1979.103.2.32.a)

30. Josef Albers
American (born Germany), 1888–1976
Formulation : Articulation, Folio II / Folder 32
["Homage to the Square"], 1972
Screenprint
15 x 20 in. (38.1 x 50.8 cm)
Mead Art Museum, Amherst College
Gift of the Alan M. Sternlieb Study Collection
(1979.103.2.33.b)

31. Josef Albers
American (born Germany), 1888–1976
Three color studies for *Homage to the Square*, n.d.
Oil on blotting paper
5 1/8 x 11 ¾ in. (13 x 29.9 cm)
The Josef and Anni Albers Foundation,
Bethany, Connecticut (1976.2.1218)

32. Josef Albers
American (born Germany), 1888–1976
Color study, n.d.
Oil on blotting paper
3 1/8 x 11 15/16 in. (7.9 x 30.3 cm)
The Josef and Anni Albers Foundation,
Bethany, Connecticut (1976.2.1374)

33. Josef Albers
American (born Germany), 1888–1976
Color study (*Homage to the Square / White Line Square*), n.d.
Oil on blotting paper
13 1/8 x 4 13/16 in. (33.3 x 12.2 cm)
The Josef and Anni Albers Foundation,
Bethany, Connecticut (1976.2.1394)

34. Josef Albers
American (born Germany), 1888–1976
Color study, n.d.
Oil on blotting paper
3 1/8 x 12 in. (7.9 x 30.6 cm)
The Josef and Anni Albers Foundation,
Bethany, Connecticut (1976.2.1471)

35. Josef Albers
American (born Germany), 1888–1976
Two color studies for *Homage to the Square*, n.d.
Oil on paper
4 7/8 x 11 5/8 in. (12.4 x 29.5 cm)
The Josef and Anni Albers Foundation,
Bethany, Connecticut (1976.2.1514)

36. Josef Albers
American (born Germany), 1888–1976
Color study, n.d.
Oil on paper
3 7/8 x 11 11/16 in. (9.8 x 29.6 cm)
The Josef and Anni Albers Foundation,
Bethany, Connecticut (1976.2.1594)

37. Josef Albers
American (born Germany), 1888–1976
Two color studies for *Homage to the Square*, n.d.
Oil on cardboard (coated side of shirt cardboard)
11 x 4 15/16 in. (27.9 x 12.5 cm)
The Josef and Anni Albers Foundation,
Bethany, Connecticut (1976.2.174)

38. Josef Albers
American (born Germany), 1888–1976
Color study for *Homage to the Square*, n.d.
Oil and graphite on blotting paper
12 x 12 in. (30.5 x 30.5 cm)
The Josef and Anni Albers Foundation,
Bethany, Connecticut (1976.2.79)

39. Richard Anuszkiewicz
American, 1930–
Annual Edition, 1970
Enamel screenprinted on masonite
8 x 6 in. (20.3 x 15.2 cm)
The Josef and Anni Albers Foundation,
Bethany, Connecticut (1994.45.100)

40. Richard Anuszkiewicz
American, 1930–
Annual Edition, 1974
Enamel screenprinted on masonite
7 ¾ x 5 1/8 in. (19.7 x 13 cm)
The Josef and Anni Albers Foundation,
Bethany, Connecticut (1994.45.103)

41. Richard Anuszkiewicz
American, 1930–
Annual Edition, 1975
Enamel screenprinted on masonite
5 1/8 x 7 ½ in. (13 x 19.1 cm)
The Josef and Anni Albers Foundation,
Bethany, Connecticut (1994.45.104)

42. Richard Anuszkiewicz
American, 1930–
Hot Pink Square, 1977
Acrylic on canvas
48 ¼ x 48 ¼ in. (122.6 x 122.6 cm)
Mead Art Museum, Amherst College,
Gift of Henry Feiwell (1978.113)

43. Richard Anuszkiewicz
    American, 1930–
    Annual Edition, 1984
    Enamel screenprinted on masonite
    7 x 5 ½ in. (17.8 x 14 cm)
    The Josef and Anni Albers Foundation,
    Bethany, Connecticut (1994.45.111)

44. Richard Anuszkiewicz
    American, 1930–
    Annual Edition, 1984
    Enamel screenprinted on masonite
    7 x 5 ½ in. (17.8 x 14 cm)
    The Josef and Anni Albers Foundation,
    Bethany, Connecticut (1994.45.113)

45. Ruth Asawa
    American, 1926–2013
    Untitled, ca. 1946–1949
    Watercolor on paper
    9 1/8 x 11 7/8 in. (23.2 x 30.2 cm)
    The Josef and Anni Albers Foundation,
    Bethany, Connecticut (1976.30.5)

46. Ruth Asawa
    American, 1926–2013
    Circles, ca. 1946–1949
    Oil on paper
    5 x 12 in. (12.7 x 30.5 cm)
    The Josef and Anni Albers Foundation,
    Bethany, Connecticut (2007.30.13)

47. Ben Chassiel (Arnold Trehub)
    American, 1923–
    Totem VI, 1974
    Heliokinetic collage
    19.5 x 19.5 x 4 in. (49.5 x 49.5 x 10.2 cm)
    Mead Art Museum, Amherst College
    Gift of the artist (2015.09)

48. J. Clement (student, Yale School of Art)
    Additive and subtractive color (color study),
    1951–1963
    Color-aid paper and construction paper on
    cardboard
    14 x 22 in. (35.6 x 55.9 cm)
    The Josef and Anni Albers Foundation,
    Bethany, Connecticut (1976.26.553)

49. Tom Geismar (student, Yale School of Art)
    American, 1931–
    Untitled (color study), 1951–1963
    Color-aid paper on cardboard
    9.5 x 14 in. (24.1 x 35.6 cm)
    The Josef and Anni Albers Foundation,
    Bethany, Connecticut (1976.26.634)

50. D. McBrayer (student, Yale School of Art)
    Vibration of colors (color study), 1951–1954
    Color-aid paper on mat board
    5 ¾ x 9 in. (14.6 x 22.9 cm)
    The Josef and Anni Albers Foundation,
    Bethany, Connecticut (1976.26.518)

51. Berit Orr (student, Yale School of Art)
    Demonstration of the Bezold Effect (color study),
    1951–1963
    Color-aid paper and construction paper on
    cardboard
    14 1/8 x 21 ¾ in. (35.9 x 55.2 cm)
    The Josef and Anni Albers Foundation,
    Bethany, Connecticut (1976.26.549)

52. Roland Peagle (student, Yale School of Art)
    Film color with the illusion of tinted overlays (color
    study), 1951–1963
    Color-aid paper on cardboard
    8 ¼ x 10 3/8 in. (21 x 25.4 cm)
    The Josef and Anni Albers Foundation,
    Bethany, Connecticut (1976.26.546)

53. Unknown (student, Yale School of Art)
    Untitled (leaf study), 1950–1959
    Color-aid paper and leaves
    5 ¾ x 5 ¾ in. (14.6 x 14.6 cm)
    The Josef and Anni Albers Foundation,
    Bethany, Connecticut (1976.26.750)

54. Unknown (student, Yale School of Art)
    Untitled (color study), 1958–1960
    Construction paper on cardboard
    14 x 22 in. (35.6 x 55.9 cm)
    The Josef and Anni Albers Foundation,
    Bethany, Connecticut (1976.26.581)

55. Unknown (student, Yale School of Art)
    Untitled (color study), 1951–1963
    Color-aid paper on cardboard
    5 ½ x 6 in. (14 x 15.2 cm)
    The Josef and Anni Albers Foundation,
    Bethany, Connecticut (1976.26.519)

56. Unknown (student, Yale School of Art)
    Untitled (color study), 1951–1963
    Color-aid paper on mat board
    14 x 22 in. (35.6 x 55.9 cm)
    The Josef and Anni Albers Foundation,
    Bethany, Connecticut (1976.26.624)

www.ingramcontent.com/pod-product-compliance
Lightning Source LLC
Chambersburg PA
CBHW051153220526
45473CB00003B/757